An Adoptee's Journey

Letters of My Life

Gaynor Cherieann

First edition printed and published in the United Kingdom 2022.

A CIP catalogue record of this book is available from the British Library.

ISBN (Paperback): 9781739157890
Imprint: Independently published
Typesetting design: Matthew J Bird

For further information about this book, please contact the author at:
gaynorcherieannauthor.wordpress.com
gaynorcherieannauthor@outlook.com

This book is dedicated
to my grandchildren,
with love forever.

Foreword

Everyone enjoys receiving a letter. Especially one written from the heart.

Some correspondence shares deep thoughts and feelings from the writer which is difficult for the reader to read. Other times, the post is pure joy.

In this book, Gaynor Cherieann couriers you through an emotional maze. Her identity, her highs and her lows are laid bare. Let her guide you. Don't judge… just read. Take a moment to feel what Gaynor felt as she wrote these words.

I promise you are about to go through the full gamut of emotions. You'll feel anger, frustration, joy, shock and even hatred can bubble inside. What rises to the surface, is somebody who needs more than simple answers and is tired of the gloss. Gaynor isn't frightened to ask difficult questions and digs deep into her heart for answers.

A warning. Some of these letters are not an easy read. But don't worry, many provide light relief, hope and joy. That's what a letter should do.

In these days of fast electronic responses, taking the time to write and read a letter is a dying art. With her permission, you're about to eavesdrop on the most open and emotive parts of her life. I know you're in for a fascinating read as Gaynor explores who she is and the roles that those around her played.

Michael Heppell
Author, Speaker, Coach

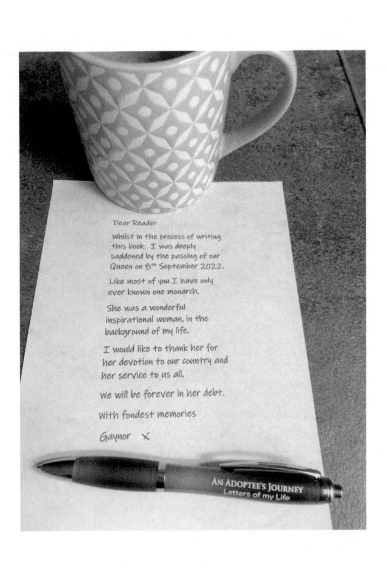

Dear Reader

Whilst in the process of writing
this book. I was deeply
saddened by the passing of our
Queen on 8ᵗʰ September 2022.

Like most of you I have only
ever known one monarch.

She was a wonderful
inspirational woman, in the
background of my life.

I would like to thank her for
her devotion to our country and
her service to us all.

We will be forever in her debt.

With fondest memories

Gaynor X

"Letters are expectations packaged in an envelope" – Shana Alexander

To Everyone Reading This

Dear Inquisitive Reader

Do you get a thrill when a handwritten envelope drops through your letterbox? Do you try to recognise the handwriting?

You slit it open with great anticipation. Someone has taken the time to write to you, it may brighten your day or bring sad news, but you are still intrigued.

Imagine you move into a new house. You open the loft space to pack away all that 'stuff', the same 'stuff' which has followed you from the last three house moves that you still haven't found the time to sort out! As you climb into the loft to push the boxes into the far corners, you spy an old shoebox, pull it out, take the dusty, slightly wrinkled box into the light, and open the lid. Inside there is a pile of letters.

These letters, of course, have piqued your interest. You go down from the loft, make yourself a cup of tea and immediately immerse yourself in somebody else's life.

Don't forget your glasses. The handwriting may be tricky; handle them with care!

This book is that shoebox.

This is my journey.

"I can't go back to yesterday because I was a different person then."
Lewis Carroll — Alice in Wonderland

To the MAA - Movement for an Adoption Apology

Dear fellow adoptees and birth parents,

Thank you for fighting for an apology from the British government for the terrible way young mothers of the past, just like mine, had to give up their babies unwillingly. They were unmarried and condemned by the authorities, the church and the wider society.

You have fought tirelessly for several years on our behalf. I recently joined the fight and hope I can see it through to the end.

It makes me cry whenever I watch the moving apology from the Australian government back in 2013 by prime minister Julia Gillard for the same reasons.

It was fantastic to get a call from the BBC to be interviewed in May 2021 to tell my adoption story. Duncan Kennedy and his cameraman, Tim were great. They came to my house and set me at ease. They needed to film me doing an activity. Tim got me to make a cake on camera and even put the small go-pro camera in with the flour for special effects. Surprisingly, the cake turned out okay! It made my family laugh as I'm not known for my cake-making abilities.

What a whirlwind of a week following that interview. I was asked to appear on a video link for BBC breakfast TV and interviewed for two different radio stations, Five Live and Capital. I remember shaking and feeling sick with fear, but I got through it and felt proud afterwards.

To say I was surprised by all the attention is an understatement. I then received a call from a Russian news station for another interview. I had a moment of panic and wanted to say no, but I took a breath and remembered why I was putting myself through all this.

The lady reporter and her cameraman insisted they needed to see me in person, although I would have been quite happy with an online interview. They travelled from London to our caravan in Wales for the interview on a bank holiday weekend. Utter madness, the actual piece lasted about fifteen minutes and my bit even less, but their journey in total took them over 8 hours.

A week later, they sent me a copy of my interview in Russian, which was fascinating to watch. Luckily, they send me a translation. I found it so interesting learning that the former 'Eastern bloc,' now the Eastern and Central European countries, did not have a system like ours; they either sent unwanted children to the state nurseries or brought them up within their wider families. I think the most surreal week of my life.

In 2022 the official gathering of evidence for the anticipated apology is progressing. Reports are being compiled and we can hope against hope our voices get heard. Harriet Harman MP is behind us and extremely supportive of our fight.

By sharing a part of my story with the press and others, I realised I wanted to tell my story in my own words, for my family and for everyone who might be interested. Here goes...

Keep up the excellent work, everyone associated with the MAA. Hopefully, I will see you on the other side.

Love, Gaynor (one of the adopted babies).

Me being interviewed by Duncan Kennedy from BBC for Documentary "If You Love Your Baby".

Me attempting to make a Victoria Sponge cake at the request of Tim the camera man.

'The world may not change if you adopt a child, but for that child, their world will change "-Unknown

To my adopted mother

Dear Beryl,

So, you're dead then?

I was informed of your death third hand. Your funeral had been and gone. I then contacted Leesa, your other daughter and other family members to let them know.

Did anyone attend? I doubt it; you didn't even have a decent word to say about anybody, did you?

Apparently, you died alone in November 2021 after a brief stay in hospital in Scotland, a place you chose to move to over twenty years ago, away from all your friends and family. What a relief when I heard the news of your death; there wasn't any sadness. As the old saying goes, "you reap what you sow".

It should have been so different. I only get upset about the past when I think about what could have been. All the lovely family occasions you missed, witnessing my amazing children become the fantastic adults they are today.

My memory of those times is sketchy. Perhaps you tried to be a good mother when Leesa and I were small, but you were happy when you were controlling people and situations. (Which is often easier with small children). You loved your dogs because they always did as they were told!

However, I would like to thank you for telling me from an early age about being adopted. An immense relief: it meant I didn't have to worry about sharing your genes and imagine growing up to be anything like you. Instead, I was able to fantasise about my real mum and who she might be.

Later in life, I learned what the word narcissist means and was shocked when reality hit me. The word's description perfectly matched your personality and traits displayed throughout my life.

Recently I read something which rang true, "You want people to hate you because hate spreads, then you have won. Only love can cut the chain."

It has been over twenty-five years since I last wrote to you by letter, trying to offer an olive branch. But to no avail.

My life has been so much less stressful without you in it.

I often thought you should have been an actress; you were brilliant at fooling those around you. "Such a lovely woman." The church crowd and people in our village would say. But they didn't live with you and had no idea. God forbid if they ever guessed Leesa and I were adopted. What would they have thought of you?

You attended church regularly and did the things that made you look virtuous. Like giving to charity, making large food platters for church functions, inviting the church folk to fancy meals at your house, helping with the Brownies and being a supportive wife to the churchwarden. Did you think that made you a Christian?

No one knew the real you, did they?

Life at home without onlookers was not all charity and kindness; was it Beryl?

Another letter arrived in January 2022 telling Leesa and I that we had been disinherited and written out of your will. To be expected, of course, but we don't know who the beneficiary is so more secrecy! How typical.

We may contest the will. We will certainly try to obtain our items that you kept from us.

Get ready for a bit of grave-turning!

Regards Gaynor

"What makes you a man is not the ability to make a child; it is the courage to raise one."
— Barack Obama

To My Adoptive Father

Dear John (I used to call you Daddy),

You were my dad, and I loved you. What a shame you were so stubborn and opinionated that you could not appreciate other people's views.

You lost out on so much. Although you tried to be a Pappy to Richard, my eldest son, you were not interested when two more boys and a beautiful little girl came along.

I was informed you had Parkinson's disease in your later years and were unwell. I was sorry to hear this, but you moved so far away from all the people you'd ever known, friends and family who cared about you, to the highlands of Scotland with no support network around you. Just the people seeking a free holiday came to visit you. Yet what brilliant family holidays we could all have shared in the beautiful part of the world you chose to live in. What a shame!

I hope you were happy with your life in Scotland before you became unwell.

Leesa and I got together on the day of your funeral; we went to the 'Land', which used to belong to our uncle. The family called it the farm. A place we thought you enjoyed spending time with Richard before you moved to Scotland.

It was a beautiful summer's day, Leesa and I stood together by the gate, shed a few tears and whispered our messages to the sky. The sun was shining, and we thought of you; we both let off a balloon and watched them fly into the distance. We had said farewell to that part of our lives and could move on without too much sorrow.

Beryl had made it very clear we were not to attend your funeral. She tried her hardest to stop us from finding out! But we did find out and sent a large wreath with all of our family's names on it, just to annoy her.

Richard was the most upset by your death. He was incredibly close to you and felt devastated at not being informed or made welcome at your funeral to say his goodbyes.

Beryl got her way, as always, right to the end, but I still hope you had a reasonable turnout. You at least deserved that.

As a Pappy to Richard, you shared many practical skills with him. He loved spending his summer holidays in Scotland with you and his Nanny. As time went on and he grew into a young man who didn't just follow your demands, the bond got broken.

Sometimes, when I think deeply, I feel you loved Leesa and me when we were young girls, but you found it impossible to let us live our own lives and become independent. It was your way or no way.

You helped me gain a love of music by listening to your records on the stereo in the lounge, 'old blue eyes' Sinatra and Perry Como. Standing on your feet to dance as a little girl, then trying to learn the quick-step to 'tie a yellow ribbon'. Where did that daddy go? He's the one I miss.

Perhaps bringing up someone else's children would always be a tough ask. I suppose some people are just not up for the task.

I hope you are at peace now.

Love From,

Gaynor (your daughter once upon a time).

"I smile because you're my sister. I laugh because there's nothing you can do about it "- Unknown

To My 'Adopted' Sister

Dear Leesa,

We survived our upbringing and did a damn good job raising our children, didn't we?

I am so glad you got back in touch with me near my fiftieth birthday in 2013. Over the last nine years, we have grown closer together and become the proper family we always should have been.

When we were growing up, mother *(Beryl)* tried incredibly hard to drive a wedge between us, always playing us off against each other. Who's laughing now?

I can no longer say the words mum or mother; the words stick in my throat, so as you know, I have referred to her as Beryl for some years now.

I'm sorry for being a horrible big sister to you most of the time, but I got to hone my excellent skills of 'chinese burns' on you.

I know we have different memories of those times; we have learned to block them out, get on with our lives and make our own mistakes.

I am not sure if you agree, but the best things for me during those early years were having Nanny, Pappy and Uncle living a few doors down the road and being part of a village. We had a comfortable lifestyle and could do most of the activities we enjoyed. We did not lack the material things in life, having money for clothes and good food, and holidays each year. We couldn't possibly be seen in dirty clothes or look unkempt.

All these things made Beryl and John appear the ideal adoptive parents; wouldn't the authorities be pleased? What a great success story we were.

Little did they know.

It is difficult to describe to people looking in from the outside.

A particular incident from childhood that sticks in my mind is when Beryl hit me with that belt with a sizeable metallic buckle that left its mark for weeks. I had the task of walking us home from school; we did not cross the road properly as we were too excited chatting and running. We ran out in front of the cars without looking, nearly getting run over. Living in a village meant everyone knew us, one of the neighbours couldn't wait to tell Beryl. Hence, I got all the blame ... I was seven.

We just accepted not being allowed to play with the other children in our street. Unable to join the village brownies because we shouldn't mix with children, from our school.

Instead, Beryl took us into town for our social activities, dancing classes, brownies, and church, which was better for her. She could put on a façade for those people who didn't see her every day.

Do you remember how we were expected to join the church choir and bellringing group, attend prayer meetings and show up at church, three times on a Sunday? I am sure you will never forget the time you got caught in the bell rope whilst bell ringing and flew into the air. It scared the life out of me; as you came back down to the floor with a massive crash and were very bruised, it could have been so much worse; I certainly did not return to that 'dangerous activity 'again, no thank you. I think you carried on for a while longer; very brave.

What about the Saturdays we spent polishing the drainpipe so we could see our reflections in it? Don't forget she made us iron the dishcloth. I bet you haven't done either of these things again in the last forty years, my dear.

Our childhood consisted of being smacked for the slightest thing, being sent to our rooms frequently and being told we were useless.

Where was the 'unconditional love' that a mother should have?

Away from home, there were some great times wasn't there? We loved brownies and guides and later performing in The Gang Show. We had some fantastic times with Auntie Freda, Uncle Ken and Susan; they were not related to us, but we called everyone auntie back then (at least with Susan being an adoptee too, made us all feel like a special gang). Do you have any idea why the parents fell out with them? My best guess is that they didn't toe the line enough or voiced their own opinion.

Good memories.

When talking to friends or an adoption group, I always say that my childhood "was fine" and brush off the question. Things simply got worse as we grew older when we started to have our own opinions, personalities, and ambitions, gaining an insight into what our parents were really like; how dare we!

I will write again soon,

Love Gaynor (your sister always)

You and Me having a professional photo taken to keep up appearances.

"As I look back on my life, I realise that every time I thought I was being rejected. I was actually being re-directed to something better" – Steve Maraboli

To My ex-husband

Dear Tony,

It seems strange writing to you after all this time; I haven't seen you for at least twelve years. I had to include you in my letters; otherwise, a chunk of my life story would be missing.

We were too young to marry at twenty-one. We didn't know who we were back then. But we were both desperate to get away from our family homes needing our independence, and it seemed the obvious way to do it was to get married.

You were my first proper boyfriend. A few kisses and cuddles backstage at the Gang Show don't count!

We started going steady at sixteen, the same age as my mum when she fell pregnant with me.

Being terrified of upsetting my parents, I just followed their rules like a little sheep, meeting all their demands and behaving like a respectable church-going girl. I was trying to be the perfect daughter they so desperately wanted.

You were seventeen and had just started an apprenticeship in jewellery repairs. Because we had met at church, my parents thought you were respectable. Which meant you were allowed to come to my house for tea. Sometimes we were even allowed in my bedroom to watch the telly, but we had to keep the door open and were constantly interrupted with cups of tea or "would you like to come and watch so and so with us".

You even joined us on family holidays; however, we were never allowed anywhere on our own. You'd have thought we were back in the Victorian times when girls were chaperoned!

My parents even organised church holidays for everyone so all our friends could come. 'Parish Camp' with a girl's tent and a boy's tent. The parents, of course, had a borrowed motor home! But we did have some great times on those holidays.

Oh, if we had just lived together and got to know each other properly, we would have realised we were not compatible. Still, it took an engagement, saving for a house, a wedding and then a baby, and unfortunately, being generally miserable before we worked it out. Big shock!

I wasn't the perfect daughter anymore; oh, the stigma of divorce. What would the church people say? Especially when they found out I was the guilty party!

At last, I had rebelled and started to emerge from the oppressive life of being controlled. The real me began to surface.

I will never regret our relationship, as our fantastic son Richard was the wonderful outcome.

What doesn't kill you makes you stronger; I had suddenly grown up and realised where I wanted my future to go; I knew my best life was still ahead of me.

Thanks for the memories,

Gaynor

"When I wrote 'Dear Fatty', I realised that sitting and writing alone is an absolute joy." – Dawn French

To Dawn French – actor and Comedian

Dear Dawn,

I loved your book 'Dear Fatty', so I thought I would nick the idea. Thanks…

The brilliant concept of how you wrote your autobiography through letters to your best friend 'Fatty,' other friends, workmates, old flames and the cat, if I remember correctly.

I hope my story will be just as heartfelt and interesting, but it won't be as funny as yours. I am not a comedian and have never fallen into a puddle right up to my middle!

The best I can manage is bursting into song at family occasions, dancing around the kitchen, falling off my bike into a rosebush (hence I never rode one again) and being well-known as the village information woman. If you want to know something, just ask me!

So, thanks for unintentionally helping me with this project and for all the laughs you continue to give,

Love Gaynor (a huge fan)

*"You are my son, my moons and my stars"-
Unknown*

To My Eldest

Dear Richard,

Hasn't your Nan (Beryl) excelled herself this time? Even from beyond the grave?

How evil was she to send you a letter to be opened after her death with nasty, spiteful lies? I know this upset you at the time, even though you tried and put on a brave face for me. Always saying you don't care, and it doesn't bother you, but I know it does.

I am so sorry I inflicted her upon you. If I could turn back time, I would have stopped the relationship with Beryl and John, your nan and pap, when I realised how toxic they were.

I genuinely thought I was doing the right thing by allowing them to stay in your life.

I think Pappy did love you in his own way. You had a pretty good relationship with him. He taught you various things and you enjoyed your time in Scotland during those summer holidays. You learnt to fish, play golf, and helped chop down trees, splitting the wood for the log burner. These skills helped you choose a career in the outdoors, climbing and cutting down trees which you love.

It has taken me countless years to realise how incapable of love Beryl was and probably the single most selfish person you could ever meet.

Why was I surprised when she, your nan, didn't tell you of your pappy's death and didn't want you at the funeral?

She then changed her 'Will' to exclude you, Leesa and me.

I should have known better. Hindsight is a wonderful thing!

They strung you along for years, telling you that you would inherit everything.

They had you running around after them, nearly killing yourself. Driving up to Scotland in a day and then demanding you work hard labour when you arrived chopping wood and clearing the garden without a break. Getting you to go to Scotland making you feel guilty by saying pappy was dying. It was lies, all lies!

I am ever so sorry I put you through all that.

Yours always,

Love Mum xx

"If I could have anyone in the world, it would still be you" - Me

To My Wonderful Husband

Dearest Paul,

You saved me.

You are my best friend and confidant. Without you, I honestly believe I would not have survived and wouldn't be the person I am today.

Our marriage would not have lasted, if we hadn't cut off the cancerous people who called themselves my parents. They were the only thing we argued about in our early marriage.

Apparently, according to them, we would not last. "You were too controlling; I should have stayed in my first marriage, poor Richard coming from a split home" and other equally nasty comments. Thank goodness you dared to stand up to them, for all our sakes.

It feels like a small chapter in our lives now, doesn't it?

Since having no contact with Beryl and John, our lives have been amazing, our four beautiful children have all grown up into fantastic adults, have partners, great jobs, and Richard has three fabulous children of his own.

You helped me find my birth family with no questions asked. Even if it had not worked out with them, I knew you would be there for me no matter what.

How lucky are we? We have had some fantastic trips abroad, a Mediterranean cruise, visits to New York and Washington DC, to name but a few. Sharing 'big' birthdays and celebrating our love at our vow renewal ceremony for our silver wedding, joined by the most important people in our lives.

We must not forget that one occasion, we were *'posh'*, going to Buckingham Palace for the Queen's Garden Party, rubbing shoulders with the elite and famous. Unquestionably, one of life's highlights!

Our life so far has been a fairy tale, my darling.

Love you forever,

Gaynor x

A wonderful time together in 2021.

Hannah Hall Photography

"A moment in my arms, forever in my heart." – Unknown

To My Birth Mum

Dear Mum,

I have so much to say to you it will probably take a few letters. Most importantly, I am happy I found you twenty-eight years ago.

We have spent those years building a relationship. Not all plain sailing, but families never are.

I do feel we are great friends now, but we both have separate issues due to the circumstances of my birth.

I have always understood why you couldn't keep me, but the hurt on all sides doesn't go away completely, does it?

All my life, I thought of meeting you and imagined what you would be like, especially on my Birthday. I felt a piece of me was missing, not knowing where I came from. Always desperately hoping I came from love.

When I received my adoption file, my detective skills worked out; you had gone on to marry my dad; how amazing! The questions in my head were endless. Did you want me to find you? What had happened in your life? Did you have more children?

Once I was sure I had found you and got your telephone number, I couldn't wait to contact you.

I was very apprehensive; I was shaking so much that Paul had to make the initial phone call. To this day, he jokes, "how many sons-in-law speak to their mother-in-law before her daughter does"?

When you told me I had two biological sisters, I felt overjoyed and thought my head would explode.

Even though you and Dad are no longer a couple to find out, at last, I had come from true love. Wow, that was all I had ever dreamed of. So many emotions I couldn't process everything.

The timings worked for us all. You and Dad were able to come to meet me within a few days of that first phone call. You were able to meet your three grandsons and share photographs of my sisters, Emma and Amy. Suddenly many things made sense. I looked like Dad; Richard's brown eyes were the same as my sisters. The jigsaw pieces were finally slotting into place.

After all these years, the time apart doesn't hurt quite so much. We try our best to just look forward to the future of our relationship now.

During the years since we met again, we have shared many family occasions: births, birthdays, weddings and funerals. I finally feel grateful to know where I came from.

We often discuss sad stories of the reunions that haven't worked out from the ITV show Long Lost Family or the stories we hear in the news and know just how lucky we are.

With all my love,

Gaynor (your baby Cherie-Ann)

Mum and Me in the beginning.

Mum as a young woman.

"Oh, what a night. Late December back in sixty-three"
- Frankie Valli and the Four Seasons

To My Birth Father

Dear Dad,

You knew I would find you. You always said, "If she has my inquisitive genes, she will come looking".

When you told me that you had taken the day off work on my Twenty-first Birthday and drove to Leicester to see if you could find me, searching the local papers, it made me feel so loved and wanted. Sadly, I wasn't in that county. As it turned out, I had never moved from my birth town. The place where you came to visit me as a tiny baby in the mother and baby home, but you had no information, just a hunch. Thanks for trying.

The day I got my birth records back in 1994 at the local council offices and met my councillor, Veronica, she handed me my file, and we slowly talked through it together.

Wham, I had another identity, Cherie Ann Ball; I don't know why I hadn't considered this. It hit me hard and took some time to process. Of course, you and mum had always thought of me as Cherie for all those years. How sad the name you lovingly gave to me was taken away.

Later, I think I cried when you told me you had named me after the Frankie Valli song 'Sherry' but changed the spelling to Cherie, the French way of spelling, meaning darling. After a couple of years of us being a family again, I had to add that special name by deed poll as my middle name to honour my true identity.

I love that song. I now listen to all of Frankie's albums; Jersey Boys is my favourite musical of all time.

You gave me the gift of music; you played in several bands over the years. I think you wanted this as a career; being so talented, it would have been amazing if this had become your vocation. Mum said you made a record once with the help of the DJ John Peel, in a band called 'Westonians'.

One of the bands you played in was the backing group for some bands who became famous. The Rolling Stones and Wizard are two of them. You both were very much into the 'sixties' music scene. In contrast, I was brought up on 50's music as my adopted parents were ten years older than you.

I suppose my arrival when you were so young changed the course of your life. It would never be the same again.

Sadly, having never seen you and mum together as a couple, I have no idea what growing up with you would have been like. I am so glad you are still great friends, which made our reunion so much easier.

Life moves on. You are re-married. I have a half-sister, Anna, whom I have only met once, but you keep that family to yourself. We all lead such busy lives.

It is great to get together a couple of times a year to catch up; I am so thankful to have found you,

Lots of love,

Your eldest daughter,

Gaynor x

You with one of your bands, you are third in from the left.

"Baby, I know the first cut is the deepest".
– Rod Stewart

To The Legend Rod the Mod
(Rod Stewart)

Dear Rod,

I have loved your music since the 'Blondes Have More Fun' album in the late 70s. I was also blonde; unlike the song, I wasn't having much fun back then; I wasn't living my best life. That LP got shared around my senior school class. Everyone taped it on their tape recorders; no wonder it was returned scratched! However, I gained a bit of street cred!

I knew you had given up a daughter for adoption. Oh, how I wished that girl had been me.

I converted my husband to your music. He grew up listening to Blondie and Kate Bush. We both adored the stage show 'Tonight's the Night' based on the songs of your early career, especially 'Sailing'.

We saw you at a concert in London about twenty years ago. It was fantastic. I brought tickets to see you again in Birmingham, but I felt ill just before entering the arena and had to go home. My family lovingly called it one of my turns! The tickets were a present from me to my husband for his birthday. I still owe him a gig. Please keep Rocking Rod so we can see you again someday.

I wasn't allowed your posters on my wall in my teens. My mother didn't approve. Rumour would have it that you were a well-known naughty boy back then. I had to keep the pictures in my bedroom drawer along with the Bay City Rollers. I did have a tartan scarf; you will be pleased to hear!

My wall had 'Cliff' and 'Donny'; the good boys displayed. What a good girl I was.

I feel your music has evolved as we all got older, and your voice is definitely sexier. I still love It; my Alexa must be sick of you.

Thanks for the great music. Keep doing what you do best.

Kind regards,

Gaynor (a lifelong fangirl) x

"If you love your baby, you will let it go to a proper family" – Quoted by many social workers of the time

My Birthday 2022

Dear Mum,

Another birthday. Thank you for the letter you included with my birthday card. You have written one every year since our reunion. Always with a special message to make up for all those years apart.

Growing up, I would always reflect on my birthday. Curious about the mum who gave me away, desperately wanting to know where I came from. I had a big hole in my heart and a sense of grief. I still struggle each year on my birthday; other adoptees will understand this and get it.

Soon we will have been back together longer than we were apart, which is fantastic. We know we are lucky. Let's celebrate. On our twentieth reunion anniversary, we went to London with Dad and Paul to watch the show Jersey boys. There were a few tears that day, many memories and some singing along if I remember correctly—what a joy to share the music of your youth and my special song.

You had such a traumatic time around my birth, so very young at sixteen. Being sent away to a mother and baby home in a strange town, giving birth alone, looking after me and bonding with me for six weeks. The social worker then took me. You were given no choices and expected to forget.

I know the experience has affected you all your life, the shame and heartache you felt. Friends shunned you. Finding it hard to talk about and unable to tell new people you meet even now. Just a handful of close friends know the truth.

I don't blame you at all. I know you wanted to keep me and loved me very much. You were given no choices and told to give me up. The pressure from family and society was immense. You didn't stand a chance of going against the system. I know Dad would have married you, but your families said you were both too young. They were all selfish people who didn't want your mistake to impact their lives.

As an only child, Dad had been a bit of a nuisance to his parents. I believe his grandma brought him up. By the time Dad had reached seventeen, they had reached a point of being able to do precisely what they wanted. They certainly didn't want anything to ruin their busy social life.

Your parents were on the verge of splitting up and going their separate ways; what choice did you have?

The mother and baby home must have been terrifying and so lonely for a young girl. You had to work hard to help with all the chores (Polishing the staircase is the job that sticks in your memory). You were lucky it wasn't an unpleasant place, and your time there was not too bad. We hear stories of terrible things happening in other homes. You said it felt like a unique girl's club away from the real world. You were all in the same boat, with so much in common.

Being a mum myself, I cannot imagine what having your baby taken from you must feel like, even in my worst nightmares. How cruel, with no counselling, advice or help offered. You were just told to get on with your life and not to discuss or dwell on it.

In this year's birthday letter, you wrote, "Although it is many years now since I went through the sadness of giving birth to you alone and our separation, it is still locked away inside my heart and will never be forgotten. The years we have been back together have eased the pain".

I have kept all the birthday letters.

All my love,

Your Cherie x

"People who are meant to be together find their way back; they may take a few detours but they're never lost" - Unknown

To Nicky Campbell, TV and Radio Presenter

Dear Nicky,

You interviewed me briefly for your radio station Five Live about the proposed adoption apology from the government.

During that time (May 2021), I was asked to participate in numerous interviews for various news outlets.

What a whirlwind week. You probably won't remember, but thanks for listening to my story.

Some years ago, I read your book 'Blue Eyed Boy' about your adoption journey. I found it so interesting; everyone's story is so unique. However, all the stories have a similar thread running through them: so many emotions, regrets and loss.

I am addicted to the 'Long Lost Family' series. Such amazing stories. You and Davina McCall do a fantastic job helping people reunite with parents, siblings, children and other family members.

The 'what happened next' episodes are so emotional. Unfortunately, it is hard to watch when reunions do not work out. Maybe this is because everyone has changed, grown-up or moved on in their lives. Reconnecting is a balance. The scales are extremely precarious, and emotions run so high. However, I don't think anyone regrets trying, as anything they find out is a bonus, especially if they knew nothing of their past.

Some mothers find it so hard. They expect to have that tiny baby back in their arms, but they are standing in front of a grown adult who has lived a whole life without them.

They just can't move forward beyond that terrible time in their lives.

Your DNA programmes are brilliant and are helping countless people to find their true identities. Keep up the excellent work, and I will keep watching. Thank you.

Kind regards,

Gaynor

"Like sand in an hourglass, I measure my life in memory of you." - Unknown

To All my Adopted Grandparents & Uncle (Beryl's Parents and Brother)

Dear Nanny, Pappy and Uncle,

Writing this today; it is St Patrick's day, reminding me this was Pappy's birthday.

I wanted to take this opportunity to thank you for my early childhood happy memories.

When I look back to those times, I remember Pappy playing cards and dominos with me, keeping sweets to share in his special cupboard. He called them 'peps'.

Nanny, I remember you attaching the meat mincer to the table in the kitchen, mincing the Sunday left-over meat. The smell of cooking disgusting tripe for your dog. Just thinking about it turns my stomach.

Thank you for sitting with me if I was ever ill and off school. Every day you did your housework in the mornings, washed and changed at lunchtime and put on a clean apron. These traits must have been from when you were in service as a young girl.

I have happy memories of helping pod peas in your garden under a homemade tent made from a clothes horse with your lovely dog, Suzie. Picking raspberries in your garden and going blackberry picking in the nearby fields, then making jam when we returned.

When I helped you do tasks which eventually became too much for you as you got older, you always gave me pocket money.

Uncle, I think of you as a quiet gentleman who worked hard for a living as a market gardener. I have happy memories of playing cards with you.

I tried to help you when you were left alone after Nanny died by doing small jobs for you. Nanny had a long life; she died in her late eighties.

I think you understood the complexities of life in our house. You always had a cheery word. After all, Beryl was your sister!

After Nanny died when I was in my late teens, you and my dad John, had a considerable falling out. I don't remember what went on, but I recall that he cut you off and didn't want anything more to do with you. You were not the type of person to have a big argument with anyone or fall out with people. Perhaps you didn't jump to his tune or disagreed with something he said or wanted.

The break-up meant you didn't feel you could attend family occasions or be in each other's company. It made life difficult for us all. You sadly missed out on so much.

I am so glad you and I were still in touch despite my dad. Thankfully Beryl didn't cut you off. However, this did cause a lot of friction between the two of them.

Life often isn't fair. You were just getting ready for retirement when you had a fatal heart attack at home. How true the statement of "life's too short"?

Having grandparents and an uncle living only four doors down the road as we grew up meant we had a special relationship. You never treated Leesa and I as anything other than your grandchildren and nieces, you all loved us in your different ways, and we loved you in return.

Thank you for some of my best childhood memories.

Love Gaynor

P.S. Pappy, I am delighted to have acquired your WW1 medals from Beryl's estate.

I will treasure them and pass them on to my children, and I am thinking about how best to display them.

On my 'bucket list' is being able to go on a battlefield tour following your personal war journey.

Pappy & Nanny

Uncle (Les)

(My other grandfather - John's Dad)

Dear Granddad,

You too, have been gone from my life way longer than you were in it, but I do remember you.

You were always a smartly turned-out 'gentleman.' Very dapper with a pencil moustache, quietly spoken and relatively subdued.

About once a month, we would pick you up on our way home from church on a Sunday to join us for Sunday lunch, but you never stayed long after we had eaten.

I remember you always came for tea on Boxing Day, and we played cards and watched TV. I don't remember much about you as a person, but I think back fondly. I'm sure you used to give Leesa and me pocket money every time you came to our house.

The atmosphere at our house was strained when you visited; Beryl didn't like you; that was obvious; you must have felt uncomfortable. We all lived our lives constantly worried in case we said the wrong thing or did something to tip the scales, and this would set Beryl off. It was like living on a knife edge.

When you died in the late 1970s, you left all four grandchildren a small amount of money; it was greatly appreciated and nice to be thought of. I saved mine in a separate account and didn't touch it until I was expecting Richard. I used the money to buy everything for my first baby. (Richard)

You split up from your wife, John's mother, just after Beryl and John married. There was no love lost there from John. That woman must not be mentioned in our house. Leesa and I never met her; she who should not be named!

I know you were a hard-working man, a bricklayer by trade and an ARP warden during the war.

As with all my grandparents, I wish I knew more about your lives. I hope this small amount of information is a small legacy to be passed on to future generations. Memories of you will live on.

Thanks for these memories.

Gaynor x

Grandad on the left. Pappy on the right.

"Family faces are magic mirrors. Looking at people who belong to us, we see the past, present and future" - Gail Lumet Buckley

To The Prime Minister

Dear Prime Minister,

Whoever you are, by the time this bill for an Apology gets put before parliament. You could still be in nappies as I write this!!

Please take this matter extremely seriously. After all the fact-gathering and interviews, some extraordinary people, both birth mums and adoptees, were brave enough to give their emotional evidence on behalf of us all.

Some MPs and officials have said, "it all happened so long ago; why dredge all that up now"?

I felt upset and shocked to hear one MP say it wasn't the government's fault, just the culture at the time, and he didn't think an apology would make any difference.

Records say half a million children were adopted during the period we refer to, the 1940s to 1970s. The exact figures of how many were taken and not given willingly are unknown, but they are estimated to be well over half of them.

The answer is that it has affected us adoptees and birth parents all of our lives. This creates a knock-on effect to the next generation.

It is such a complicated and complex issue to comprehend if you are not directly involved.

There is so much loss for all parties involved. The adoptee's loss of not growing up with their birth mum and being a member of their natural family, understanding our genes and familial traits and looking like someone else. The birth parents' loss has been recognised as a type of bereavement.

Please do the right thing, apologise, and offer support for those still suffering, who either need counselling or help to find their relatives. Is this too much to ask?

Thank you,

Gaynor (one of the adoptees)

'A Godmother is a gift sent from above – a guardian angel that was chosen to love"

To My Godmother

Dear Auntie Margaret,

I try not to thank Beryl and John often for anything, but I will thank them for making you, my godmother. You are the epitome of what a godmother should be.

You have always been there for me, remembering my birthdays and everything happening in my life.

You are a true Christian lady, praying for me when you felt I needed it but not forcing religion on me.

When Leesa and I were children, we often came to your house for meals and went on a few family holidays together, including parish camp. We grew up with your girls, who were a little bit younger than us; they felt like cousins and were my bridesmaids when I married Tony.

We have become friends over the years, and I enjoy going out for lunch with you and Uncle Paul now and then.

I knew how privileged I was to have you as my Godmother, so I asked you to be Katie's godmother, along with Uncle Paul as her godfather. Katie recently thanked me for giving her such wonderful godparents; I know she thinks the world of you, like an extra set of grandparents.

If my memory serves me right, Beryl and John were godparents to one of your daughters, possibly Erika, your eldest. They certainly didn't set any good examples. Unfortunately, no one can see into the future, and you just do what feels right at the time, don't you?

I have tried to use your fantastic example with my two godchildren over the years.

I hope I succeeded, but that's for them to say, not me.

I know you found it difficult when Beryl and John cut you out of their lives. You could not understand what you had done. I can assure you that you did nothing wrong and were just joining a long list of excommunicated friends and family.

You moved on and have lots of supportive friends, family and neighbours around you; you didn't miss them!

To end this letter, I want to thank you for everything.

I hope you stay well and we continue to have years of friendship, love, and going out for lunch.

Gaynor. (Your goddaughter)

"Be yourself, people don't have to like you,
and you don't have to care' – Unknown

To the Excommunication club

Dear All,

You had no idea you were in this exclusive club, did you?

How lucky you are.

You belong to a free club with no membership fee, AGM, boring meetings or minutes to type up.

On the downside, there are no medals, certificates or awards either. Even though you certainly deserved the latter for all the miserable things you had to endure.

All you had to do to meet this club's criteria was to upset, irritated or disagree with Beryl and John.

This club membership goes back decades. It is an old institution. There are probably members I do not even know about or remember!

I started to list the people I thought were in this club, and then I stopped as the list began to get too long.

I knew I would miss people off.

You are friends we knew well, going on holiday together, most of you came to our house for meals, as Beryl loved to cook. Neighbours who had helped look after the dogs or cut the grass and kept an eye on the house. Plus, people like mothers of Leesa's and my friends, relatives on both sides of the family and church associates.

Most of you lovely people in the club just thought you were helping, caring and doing what a friend should do.

I won't name names because some of you are still in my life and may read this one day; what you don't know can't hurt you.

I am sure most of you are not worried you were in this club and just got on with your lives.

Wondering what you had done or said did upset a few of you, I know. I hope that knowing you were not alone and my joke about being part of a club makes you smile.

Take care, sending lots of love,

Gaynor x

The Tides of Providence - Patience Strong - poet

It's not what you gather but what you sow,
That gives the heart a warming glow,
It's not what you get but what you give,
Decides the kind of life you live.

It's not what you have but what you spare.
It's not what you take but what your share
That pays the greater dividend
And makes you richer in the end.

It's not what you spend upon yourself
Or hide away upon a shelf
That brings a blessing for the day
It's what you scatter, by the way

A wasted effort, it may seem
But what you cast upon the stream
Comes back to you recompense
Upon the tides of providence.'

To Joan, My Guide Captain

Dear Captain,

Although you died quite some years ago, you are remembered fondly.

You were our version of Miss Jean Brodie without the sex bits. Quick, block your ears!

There is a big group of women who owe you so much. Without your influence, we would not be the strong, confident, caring women we are today.

You were a true Christian lady, our guiding star.

At guides, we always sang 'grace', said prayers and read moving reflections from Patience Strong.

You were always calm and unflustered. We hardly ever saw you get cross, but we behaved ourselves not because we were scared of you but because we didn't want to disappoint you.

It was character-building. Learning all those life skills, following a set of rules, and being brought together with so many different types of girls and women.

The practical skills we learned at guides have shaped our everyday lives and will stay with us always. Most of us could still survive a few days without electricity, with a single tap, living in a tent and cooking on an open fire.

One memory that sticks in my mind from an annual guide camp is when we girls all wanted to go to the Radio 1 roadshow. It wasn't far from our campsite, just up the road and within walking distance.

Persuading you to let us go felt momentous. Of course, you didn't even know what a roadshow was, a far too modern concept for you. But after us doing extra jobs and making many promises, you said yes.

We girls talked about it for years afterwards.

One of those things people ask is, where were you when you heard Elvis had died? I clearly remember that it was the summer of 1977. We were on our annual guide camp in the Lake District; I wasn't a huge fan, but some girls cried. At least you knew who Elvis was.

I did love campfire singing; what great fun. I still have my campfire songbook, and when my children were small, I taught them many of those songs. We would sing them at bedtime before they quietened down for a story. You will be delighted to know many of those songs which have been updated are now popular at mums and tots' singing groups.

On our annual summer guide camps, Leesa and I could be ourselves.

We made lots of friends and have such fond memories. Daily tasks were cooking on the open fire, making gadgets out of wood, cleaning dixies which were black and needed to be silver again for your inspection and emptying the 'lats', the port-a-loo to the uninitiated.

Captain, you always brought your lovely mum to camp with us. She stayed in a local B & B and joined us at camp daily along with our bus driver Les. In those days, we kept the 52-seater coach for the entire twelve-day camp 'creepy Les" (our nickname for him) spent all his days at camp 'watching us'. We all called your mum 'Mum'. I never did know her real name.

What a shame Beryl and John had to muscle in and come along to our first camp in Dorset.

Typical of them interfering in our lives. After that camp, Leesa got a good telling off for telling people we were adopted when the other girls said we didn't look alike.

I often recollect your favourite saying at camp after a torrential downpour, "this is the clearing up shower." We had a lot of clearing-up showers, didn't we, Captain? It showed what a positive person you were. Of course, sometimes it actually was the clearing-up shower!

I still have my cuddly womble Orinoco that you made for me; My daughter Katie also loved playing with him.

Captain, thank you for being there for me and setting us girls a fantastic example.

Love

from Gaynor.

PS: Proud to be one of your Queens guides

My Queen's Guide Presentation 1977. Captain (far left) me, Alison and Lieutenant
(far right)

*"Some friendships are like diamonds -
timeless and unbreakable"
- Our mindful life. co*

To the ladies I worked with in my first job at Hampden Test Equipment

(I think of you as my work Mum's Dorothy and Sue)

Dear Dorothy,

You were my first work friend; I had no idea what leaving school and starting work would be like. What a big shock, but you helped me adjust as your office junior.

You took me under your wing. I learned so much from you; not only basic office skills but how to deal with the bosses and the 'cheeky chaps' on the shop floor, a big learning curve for a naive church-going girl.

It wasn't long before we became friends; I enjoyed our lunch hours together, always chatting and often popping to the chippy. I had never had an older friend before, but you taught me age doesn't matter; it has nothing to do with friendships.

When we worked together, you had a grown-up family, grandchildren and lots of life experience.'

We talked about all sorts of things. Thank you for being a great mentor.

I often cried on your shoulder about my parents and being able to unload to someone who understood helped enormously.

You met Beryl and John several times whilst we worked together. Like most people, you didn't warm to them, finding them stuck up. I know you felt all that church stuff must have been completely suffocating. In return, they didn't understand our friendship and were jealous.

After you left your job at Hampden, where we worked together, I was so glad we kept in touch by letter—keeping each other updated on our family news and enclosing photographs. You were overjoyed when

I told you of my reunion with my birth parents and couldn't wait to see pictures to look for any likenesses.

I kept all your letters for years, re-reading them occasionally.

After your husband Oliver died, you moved to be near one of your daughters. We still stayed in touch.

I remember visiting you in Nuneaton and taking you out for lunch. It is a memory I hold dear.

At your funeral, your daughters made a special mention of our friendship, which made me cry. It was a lovely heart-warming gesture.

I felt extremely privileged that you shared a special personal family secret with me, which I will take to my grave.

Thank you for all your support and help when I needed it in my life.

Your good friend

Gaynor x

"A friend is like a good bra – hard to find, supportive, comfortable, always lifts you up, makes you look better and is close to your heart!" - Unknown

Dear Sue,

You would have laughed out loud at that quote …

How funny that you arrived at the same company two years after Dorothy. You couldn't have been more different, but we got on extremely well.

Looking back in hindsight, was I searching for the mother figure I hadn't had?

Your grown-up children were just around my age. I think of you as a trendy working mum who loved her family. I was impressed by how your happy marriage to Alan in later life helped you become an independent lady. I got the impression your first marriage was stifling.

You treated me like an equal. I was grateful at that time as this was what I needed in my life.

Thank you for lending me your copy of 'Not a Penny More, Not a Penny Less", the first Jefferey Archer novel I read; you got me hooked. You introduced me to different types of music and TS Elliot's poem.

Years later, when I watched a production of 'Cats', I thought of you. What a brilliant cultural learning process you offered me, unlike the teachers from my school days.

Back then, I remember you were the one person who was sceptical about my relationship with Tony. Suggesting in a friendly way that perhaps we were too young, admitting that you had made the mistake of marrying too young. You tried to advise me quietly, but I wasn't listening; we never do when we are young and think we know everything.

You still came to our wedding sitting in church with all the chaps from work. Pete had just arrived straight from the airport with his duty-free in a carrier bag, looking like a wino with the bag clanking at his feet.

All of you couldn't wait to tell me later. We all laughed about it when I returned to work after my honeymoon. Of course, I didn't notice any of this at the time.

We stayed friends after I left that job, keeping in touch at Christmas with our newsletters. You stayed at Hampden for a few years after I left and kept me in the loop with all the gossip.

After a few years, I realised I needed to move on from my first job and gain more experience. I went to work for World Vision until I had Richard. It was the start of a long succession of jobs working for registered charities, which I still do now.

Years later, your lovely husband Alan contacted me when you were diagnosed with a brain tumour.

Paul and I were married by then. We drove to visit you at your home, I am so glad we did, but it was an incredibly upsetting time.

However, I remember something you used to say to me "marriage the second time around is best; you know what you are doing," and of course, you were right.

You were taken too young, my dear friend.

Sending heavenly love,

Gaynor x

'A Grandma is someone who plays a part in all the treasured memories we hold within our heart"-Unknown

To My Mother-in-Law

Dear Mary,

I rarely call you mum because I have two myself; it is easier to refer to you as Grandma or Paul's mum.

Thank you for being a helpful mother-in-law. We have never been close, but you have helped in many practical ways over the years.

When the children were young, you still worked full-time. You were forty-eight and on your own, due to Paul's dad (your husband), Mick, having died young. It must have been very hard.

Being just twenty when you had Paul, your eldest, meant you were a young grandma.

You were never the cuddly sitting-in-a-rocking chair type of grandma, but you were brilliant at making things, doing activities and taking the kids out for trips.

You helped with looking after the children as they grew up, often having one of them individually overnight. When you worked for Age Concern running the day centre in our village, we got to see you weekly for a cup of tea and a catch-up.

Adam and Katie remember when you took them on canal boat trips from Stoke Bruerne and visited the llamas on a farm with your day centre group. Thanks to these trips, Adam now has a canal boat of his own.

I think you enjoyed the weekend we went to Belgium to visit the war graves. What a moving but enjoyable experience, especially the last post at the Menin Gate. I definitely want to go back one day and do another tour.

I realise life has been difficult for you for various reasons. Sadly, you are now suffering from the horrible condition of dementia.

I'm not sure you will ever get to read this, but I wanted my children and grandchildren to remember you as the kind, helpful, artistic and skilled seamstress who loved her grandchildren in her unique way.

Thank you for being you.

Gaynor x

You and Mick. (My in-laws)

"Adoption is not the call to have the perfect rosy family; it is the call to give love, mercy and patience." - Graciousquotes.com

To Members of the Milton Keynes adoption support group

Dear Jan, Trish, Linda and all the other members of the group.

Our group has been a lifeline.

A secure space to discuss our feelings and issues regarding the adoption triangle: The birth family, the adopted family, and the adoptees. Three sides of the triangle.

I missed having the opportunity to attend our face-to-face meetings during the Covid lockdown and struggled to connect with you all during our forced online meetings. They seemed impersonal and too remote to me.

I feel like an old veteran at the meetings, having been reunited with my birth family for over twenty-five years. During that time, I have learnt a few things about the issues people have struggled with over the years. I hope my experience can help others occasionally.

Our adoption group works well because we have a combination of adoptees and birth parents, with the occasional adoptive parent joining us. We all bring such amazing stories to the group.

When someone new arrives, I am sure we always make them welcome. At last, they are no longer feel alone with their struggles; we all understand.

After the national lockdown, meeting up again was fantastic and catching up with everyone's news. We chatted well past the finishing time. Linda giving me a lift has been brilliant; we can talk longer and dissect the whole evening.

How amazing that one new lady in our group was looking for an adult adoption group on the internet, managed to find our group and travelled from Birmingham to join us. I hope we helped her.

During our recent meeting, when we went around the room introducing ourselves and explaining our link to adoption. I am always intrigued to see how other adoptees in the group didn't have a great adoption, the exception being Stephen. We always say things like, it wasn't great and move on quickly, not wanting to go into detail.

Of course, many people have had brilliant adoptions, like my friend Janet T. She grew up feeling loved and cherished. I fondly remember her mum and dad; they were lovely.

I have realised that shared experience brings you closer, and groups of like-minded people work well.

I hope our group can continue helping people for years to come.

All our members are eager for the adoption apology from the government, which is still moving slowly. The report is being presented anytime now and should be ready before the end of this year, 2022.

Some amazing birth mums and adoptees have told their stories to the parliamentary panel. The tears spilt over watching the emotional, brave testimonies, and I am sure you all were too.

I am looking forward to seeing you all at the next face-to-face meeting.

Sending my love to you,

Gaynor

"God does not call the qualified, He qualifies the called" - Motto of the Order

To The Nuns - The Daughters of the Holy Spirit Order

Dear Sisters,

You now live in the former Mother and Baby Home; my birthplace, this is your provincial house.

It is incredible that this lovely Edwardian house still exists and hasn't been turned into flats or sold for monetary gain.

I am so lucky to be able to visit the place of my birth. Thank you for showing me around your home, where I spent the first six weeks of my life.

Eighteen years ago, just after my sister Amy's wonderful wedding, a lovely family occasion. I was feeling very emotional and quite low. It hit me how unfair it was that I didn't grow up in my birth family and what I had missed. I realised I was driving past the end of your street on my way to an appointment. I can't describe the feeling; a wave of something came over me and suddenly, I just needed to see where I was born.

I sat outside your house for a few minutes with butterflies in my tummy, trying to pluck up the courage to knock on the door. Taking a big breath, I got out of the car and thought, I need to do this.

One of your lovely sisters opened the door and wasn't surprised at my request to look around.

Over the years, you have welcomed lots of us 'babies' desperate to learn where we were born and also birth mothers remembering or trying to get some closure—how upsetting it must have been for them and your sisters.

I felt overwhelmed standing in the large entrance hall. It took my breath away, my eyes filled, knowing my mum had walked in there, heavily pregnant later to leave with empty arms.

The beautiful wooden staircase, which my mum tells me had to be polished daily, is still the focal point as you enter.

One of the sisters kindly gave me a tour of some of the rooms and allowed me to spend a few minutes of reflection in the chapel. Thank you for allowing me a peaceful moment to gather myself. When the time came for me to leave, you said I could come back anytime.

About a year after my visit, I contacted you to arrange to bring my mum and dad.

Visiting together felt like a healing experience for all three of us. My mum had tears in her eyes, and my dad went quiet. We were finally together again in the place where they said goodbye all those years ago, thinking they would never see me again. It was a very surreal, moving experience; I well up just thinking about it.

I remember an episode of 'Long Lost Family' also filmed at your home when two birth sisters were reunited.

I recorded the episode to keep for posterity. 'That is my birth home,' I screamed at the television screen to anybody who could hear me.

When I started writing this letter in my book to you sisters, I thought I would love to go to the house again and perhaps you would let me take a few photographs. Sister Eileen was delighted at my request, and we spent a delightful couple of hours enjoying a cup of tea and chatting. Then she showed me around again, including the garden; I felt a real sense of peace and a sort of closure.

Thank you again for helping me slot another piece of my life's jigsaw into place.

With love,

Gaynor (Baby Cherie)

Front of the house	*Back of the house and garden*

Staircase	*Chapel*

"When travelling life's journey, it's good to have a sister's hand to hold on to" - Unknown

My 'Adopted' Sister

Dear Leesa,

I thought I would write again in March 2022 as we are still trying to come to terms with being disinherited.

I am baffled by trying to uncover more details of the beneficiaries of Beryl's will and trying to make sense of what went on in Scotland.

When this is all over, I will need closure by visiting Scotland to see 'Riverside', their cottage.

I think meeting the executors to thank them for everything they have done and finding out who is living in the house may help.

I hope we can do this together and you can show me where you used to live and parts of your life that I missed out on when we were not in touch for the ten years you lived there.

Talking of missing out, can you believe you had three weddings, no funerals, thank goodness, and I didn't attend any of them, and I had three, and you came to them all!

When you married Jim, still under the parent's spell, I was forbidden to attend; always trying to win favour with our parents, I duly agreed. You were the one who was out of the picture then; hence no family members were there for you that day. 'If only' is a useless thing to say, isn't it?

When you married Bren, the opposite occurred. You were the one in favour, which meant they attended your wedding—me being out of favour at that time, therefore not invited. I didn't like him anyway, so no skin!

When you married for the third time, having moved back to Leicestershire, we were not back in touch after the long break in our relationship. You did have your beautiful girls by your side on that day.

But it wasn't long after that wedding that you reached out to me and got back in touch, thank goodness.

In reverse, when I married Tony, far too young at twenty-one. But being that obedient, church-going girl, I did the expected thing, the big white wedding in church.

The church where we both sang in the choir, rang the bells and were practically part of the furniture.

What an obedient girl I was. I was marrying a boy from church and following the parents' rules by not living together before marriage, saving frantically for a mortgage, not going out and enjoying life or getting to know each other. That worked well, didn't it?

On that day thirty-eight years ago, you were by my side as my maid of honour; weren't we all so young and naive? Blimey, thirty-eight years that makes me feel old. Oh yes, I am!

Five years later, I married Paul, the love of my life, at the Towns registry office wearing a suit and hat.

We had a small intimate wedding with 25 people and the reception on a narrowboat. On that beautiful hot August day, you were there with Jim.

The parents managed to 'attend' just! I remember having to jump through a few hoops beforehand. Uncle didn't feel able to attend due to the rift between him and John. What a shame; bless him.

Then my number three 'Wedding' when Paul and I renewed our vows for our Silver Wedding. We went all out and had the works 'we did it our way'.

We invited only special people with who we wanted to share our day.

Another hot August day, with a beautiful service at the village church and reception in the village hall.

I wore an ivory wedding dress, and my darling Katie was my bridesmaid. At last, the wedding of my dreams to the man of my dreams.

What a fantastic day made even better by being able to have our children and my birth parents share our special day.

Richard walked me to the church, and Chris and Adam gave speeches.

I felt privileged to have David perform the service. He is one of my oldest friends from those church days of our youth. I had no regrets on that beautiful day, just a slight disappointment that my sister Amy and family could not come from America. But they did Skype us at the reception.

You shared our day, and we felt like a proper family with your Girls and hubby; it was fantastic to share it with you all.

What a strange sister relationship we have had over the years, but then we don't do normal!

Let's get old together, my sister.

We don't want people saying, "what a lovely old lady" we want them to say, "Oh crap, what is she up to now?"

Love and hugs,

Gaynor x

Here we are together celebrating Katie's wedding. These were the best I could find of us together as adults. We need to get better at taking photos!

Hannah Hall Photography

110

"You can't change someone who doesn't see an issue in their actions" - Unknown

To Adopted Mother

Dear Beryl,

I decided never to write you another letter but having just finished reading "Survival without Roots", a memoir written by Anna Anderson, a fellow adoptee, I have changed my mind. Her brilliantly written book unleashed many forgotten memories for me. Her adopted mother sounds just like you were all those years ago.

You were being a social climber and trying to get us to pronounce words correctly really fitted your description. The people you grew up around were not good enough anymore, and you needed to move up the social ladder.

I also realised that when you disagreed or fell out with friends and family, which was frequently, you always expected everyone around you to choose sides. Leesa and I spent our lives picking whose side we were on. It was exhausting.

If I say 'The League of Pity, 'people would gasp now at that terrible name. An organisation to help children less fortunate. Now called the NSPCC, you enrolled us into this organisation; it made you look compassionate, didn't it?

Leesa and I regularly attended gatherings like fundraisers at a local church hall and a big occasion at a ballroom in town once a year. We joined in the fancy-dress competitions, and you roped all our well-to-do friends from dancing classes. We won first prize when we went as Henry VIII and his six wives. The costumes took weeks. I went as Catherine Howard, with Leesa went as Catherine Parr. Our dad made us the costumes as using the sewing machine was second nature to him, wasn't it, being an upholsterer.

I kept that costume for dressing up for years.

You organised a concert in our garden for the same cause. We sold tickets to the neighbours, friends from dancing, brownies, and school. One of our schoolteachers even came. Why did we think us warbling 'Puff the Magic Dragon was entertainment? But it made you 'look' admirable in the local society by doing charitable things.

I have no memory of you ever saying you were proud of me. When I got presented with my Queens Guide award, I think you were proud, but you didn't say so; you had pushed me hard to get that award, so thank you.

You weren't even a proud grandparent; you were delighted when I had Richard because that meant another person you could mould and control, but you didn't think I should have any more children, and you were not interested in the others.

Finding out not long ago that you were still in contact with Tony, Richards's dad, what a surprise that was. You never stopped criticising and complaining about him during my marriage to him! How two-faced you were!

Enough of this. It just upsets me if I think too deeply about how things were, especially how they could have been.

Regards,

Gaynor (your estranged adopted daughter).

Fancy Dress, Henry VIII, and his Six Wives. Me as 5th Wife (Catherine Howard) and Leesa as 6th Wife (Catherine Parr).

115

"Sons are the anchors of a mother's life" – Sophocles

To my Eldest Son

Dear Richard,

I hope you know how much I love you. I am so proud of the wonderful man you have become and such a brilliant dad and stepdad.

We had some shaky times in your youth but nothing too drastic. With my love, your dad Paul's guidance and faith in you, everything turned out great.

It is a shame your relationship with your dad, Tony, didn't work out, but that's his loss. I know you tried to reach out to him a few times since you became a dad. For whatever reason, he did not want a relationship with you. Thankfully you don't need him. You have a dad who brought you up; I know you think the world of him.

You have struggled with relationships yourself, possibly because of coming from a split home. Maybe you don't remember living with your dad, as you were just four years old when our marriage broke up.

Getting into the wrong relationships at an early age seems to be a family trait. You became a dad for the first time, far too young with a girl you didn't love. When you were younger, you were immature. All the mates you brought home were quite a bit younger than you. In your early twenties, you were still hanging out with teenagers. Even now, you prefer the company of the younger lads you work with, but sometimes you can be led down a path, not always best for you.

When your daughter Lily came along in 2008, you were not ready to be a dad or a partner to Joanna. What happened is not my story to tell, but I hope she is happy, and perhaps we may meet her again one day. I know it is your biggest regret not being able to have a relationship with her or be a part of her life.

You stepped up when you met your lovely Rochelle and took on her two great kids, Lia, now sixteen and Maisen, ten.

Then together, you have gone on to have our delightful Jaxon, now six, Willow, five and baby Ashdon, born this year, 2022. What a busy life you all have.

I think being the eldest of four in our family prepared you a bit. You were always a brilliant big brother having patience and helping the others, teaching Katie to ride a bike and taking the blame sometimes for the antics that went on, the ones I wasn't supposed to know about!

I love it when you all get together and stories get shared. Pellet guns, climbing over the back gate late at night, and various breakages are just a few. We always had a house full of children, especially during my childminding years; you were always a brilliant help.

As your family grows, I hope you remember who you are, a kind, sensitive soul underneath the bravado.

Rochelle will be there by your side if you let her. You make a great couple and are doing a brilliant job as parents.

But remember, children don't come with a manual it is hard work; you can simply do your best.

I love you – I didn't understand real love until I had you.

Your Mum always xxxx

"Sisters are different flowers from the same garden" -Unknown

To my birth sisters, Emma and Amy

Dear Both,

I never guessed or dreamed I would have two full sisters when I started my search for my birth mum.

It must have been strange when suddenly an older sister appeared, especially for Emma, as you had always thought of yourself as the eldest. Even though mum had talked about me, I don't think you thought I would ever be part of your family.

Not growing up together has caused us various issues; we don't have any history or shared stories. Although we share genes, it doesn't mean we are alike, but we have similarities in appearance, making me feel part of the family. At last, I look like someone else. The whole nature versus nurture thing is complex, but I am forever happy I found you.

Emma, we have struggled over the years to build a relationship. We have come to an understanding now that we can talk if it concerns mum. Otherwise, we will just get on with our lives, especially since you moved to live in Minorca.

Amy, although you are sixteen years younger than me, the same age gap as mum and me, I feel we have the most in common. We are alike in a few ways, I think. We both have children, so we have a shared understanding of being mothers. I wish you lived nearer so I could be a proper Auntie to your darling children, Evan and Sophie. I haven't even met Sophie; she is now six years old!

I feel robbed of my real family, but life has so many twists and turns; I am pleased I know my history.

Anyway, you wouldn't have wanted me as your big sister growing up because I was bossy, a goody-two-shoes and excellent at "Chinese burns", according to Leesa.

So pleased we are in touch, and I came to both of your weddings with my family. I am glad we can follow each other's lives via Mum and Facebook.

Amy, I do hope you can come to England again before too long. The USA feels so far away and none of us are getting any younger. Wow, the big sixty next year for me.

Love and hugs,

Big Sis Gaynor

Emma's Wedding to James (2002)
Left to Right: Me, Emma, Amy

Amy's Wedding to Steve (2004).
Left to Right: Emma, Amy, Me

"The only thing better than me having you as my husband is our children having you for a dad." - Unknown

To my Husband of 33 years

Darling Paul,

In our first year of marriage, we broke a few of life's stress rules. Getting married, you lost your lovely dad, we moved house, and I became pregnant.

We never do things by halves!

It seems so strange now that you were Tony's friend and he introduced us. You'd spend time with him doing scouting activities, weekends away, hiking and socialising. He preferred to be away from Richard and me– but he hadn't grown up! Had he?

You often came around to our house for meals and scout meetings. Eventually, you moved into the spare room, becoming our lodger.

You were our second lodger, Lindsay being our first. Tony and I hadn't been married long when Lindsay came to stay whilst her new house was being completed. Lindsay's family were friends with mine from dancing classes when we were young. I introduced Lindsay to Tony. She attended our wedding, and we shared meals at each other's houses. Like us, Tony and Lindsay have been married for over thirty years. It's laughable looking back; you couldn't make it up.

There was an instant attraction between us, which soon grew into love—what a stressful time in the beginning. I left my marriage to Tony; you supported me and helped with Richard; we got through the bumps.

Surprisingly my parents didn't cut me off. They were extremely scathing and disappointed; because they didn't want to lose Richard, they put up with the situation.

We married a year later, moving into our first home with Richard.

Still trying to keep on the right side of my parents, we dutifully bought a small maisonette in the same village as them, not doing what we wanted, which was to rent until we could afford a family home.

Then the bottom dropped out of the housing market, causing us financial issues for years to come.

We kept our wedding small, around twenty people at the town's registry office, but it suited us at the time.

Family members still talk about how we arranged surprise transport for everyone, using minibuses from both of our parent's homes to the registry office and then to a secret location for our reception.

A narrowboat, 'The Saucy Sue', took us on a trip up the canal for two hours and then back; Richard, the only child, loved it. We did it our way but always knew we would have the 'big do' in church for our silver wedding anniversary.

I hope I supported you when your dear dad was diagnosed with cancer. He died within a few months, aged just fifty. Bless him; how he would have loved his grandchildren. Our boys have one of his traits of being able to 'talk the hind legs off a donkey" I know you still miss him, but the pain has eased with time. You were extremely close; you worked with him and shared a variety of hobbies.

He taught you how to fish and gave you a career. The family business he started, which still carries his name, has served us well, bringing up our family.

I know it still upsets you when you think back that my parents didn't even attend your dad's funeral. But then they couldn't even make any effort to attend their goddaughter's funeral, so what is there left to say?

When you reached the milestone of '50', which was a massive relief for you but bittersweet knowing you would grow older than your dear dad.

The relationship with your mum has always been tricky; you have never been close, but she has been a brilliant Grandma to our kids. They all think fondly of her. Complicated issues in recent years have made the relationship even more difficult, with her struggling health issues and her long-term partner.

I know you feel you should do more, but it is not as easy as all that.

Your family has never been close; losing your dad when you and your brothers were all just out of your teens has taken its toll.

Please remember, my darling, there is no such thing as a 'normal' family!

Your loving wife always,

Gaynor xxxx

Our beautiful Silver Wedding

"Be Brave. Be Silly. Be your own magic.
Be present. Be full of surprises.
Be adventurous. Be Kind. Be free. Be you."
— Ashita Kunjadia -an Indian poet

To My Second Son, Christopher

Dear Chris,

Bet you thought I'd never get round to writing to you? Well, firstly, you know how proud of you I am for going to university, earning a degree and securing the job of your dreams, buying your own home and working so hard.

A few health issues recently have made things quite difficult, but you have a lovely partner in your Katy. She is like another daughter to us. She worships the ground you walk on; I hope you will ask her to be your wife one of these days.

You were by far the most difficult of my babies, arriving five weeks early. I don't think you stopped crying for six months! Sickly, colicky and an all-around nightmare, how I managed to forget and have more children, I don't know. I must have been on drugs, or perhaps it was the alcohol!

As a child, you were constantly at the doctor's or visiting A & E. You still have a Harry Potter scar to show for your escapades. You worshipped Richard and became a brilliant big brother to the others, with no jealousy, just sharing and helping.

You didn't get on with Beryl and John, your so-called grandparents; no love lost there. Beryl never forgave you for saying, "it always rains in Scotland," when you were nine. Hence, they never invited you to join Richard for the summer holidays. I don't think it affected you long-term; you were a bit sad about it as a child, but I am pleased I didn't inflict them upon you. You are all the better for it; I'm sure you agree.

Yvonne, one of our family friends, was always convinced you would come out to us as gay. Her daughter Megan was your best friend in primary school. When you and Megan played 'weddings', you were the one who dressed up as the bride. Everywhere you went, you always wanted to do the hoovering; at her house, our home and mums and tots, no one else got a look in. Even now, years later, you always want to try out someone's new hoover; perhaps you missed your vocation as a hoover tester.

Having said that, others thought you would be an entrepreneur. This stems from my sister Emma's wedding. Each table had pens and paper to write answers to a quiz. Sometime later, you collected all the pens from the tables; wow, that's helpful, I thought! You then encouraged your brothers to go with you to each table, selling the pens back to the guests; you made everyone laugh, plus a bit of money on the side. Impressive or what?

Like most of us in our family, you had a few rocky early relationships because you were either too young or attracted to the wrong person. Still, I think you have found your soulmate in Katy. She has been brilliant during your health issues and needs a medal for putting up with you. Leaving lights on and cupboards open is your forte. As for putting stuff away or doing a job at home, you will do it when you're ready, usually at least three hours later, hoping someone will have already done it!

It's a good job; your dad and brothers can help with practical tasks. I think you can paint a wall under duress and tighten a loose screw, but that's the sum of your DIY skills. Just stick to fast pursuits on the motorway and arresting drug dealers, which is what you are best at.

It's fantastic when a parent can say they enjoy spending time with their adult children because they get on so well. That's how I feel about you and Katy.

Before I sign off, I would like to thank you for your support regarding this book; it went something like this-

"Well, if you have a load of copies left over, we can always sell them at your funeral to help pay for it. "

Love you forever,

Your Mum x

My Son -

*Never feel that you are alone. No matter
how near or far apart.*

I am always right there in your heart.

*Just believe in yourself and remember you
only fail when you stop trying.*

*Never forget whatever you go through; no
matter what, I will always love you.*

- Life Learned Feelings

To Adam, my Third son

Dear Adam,

Your turn for a letter now!

You truly are one of a kind, and I know lots of mothers say that, but it is so true when it comes to you. You make us all laugh with your dramatic stories and the incidents that constantly happen to you.

'Just you'!

However, I often feel you have drifted away from our family, but I suppose that is natural when you grow up, start your own life and move away. I hope you know how much we all love you and your unique ways.

You were the perfect baby and child, a strong, determined character who instantly adored your new baby sister. With only twenty-two months between you, you grew up being inseparable.

You were such a sensitive soul playing with teddies long after other boys your age. You didn't like sports but enjoyed the outdoors; biking and camping were your thing. You loved cubs and scouts and later became a brilliant cub leader. The kids adored you, giving you the nickname 'Flopsy'; not sure I ever got to know why or want to!

I think you just about reached your ambition of standing on most of the world's continents before you were twenty-one, apart from the arctic ones. I can't remember all the fantastic trips you have taken, but you made us so proud by travelling to Australia on your own at sixteen. That first trip set you off on your adventures.

When you got your first motorbike, I was scared, as all mothers would be, but you did the training and got the proper licence, so I had to accept you knew what you were doing. You love it and have had many great trips in this country and abroad. You still have a great passion for days out on your own, just the bike and the road.

At seventeen, when you told us you were gay, I was initially shocked but not surprised. I hope your dad and I have always supported you and welcomed any partners.

Thank goodness Beryl and John were not in our lives at that time. They would not have understood or accepted you. Being biased, religious and from an older generation. All other family members were so welcoming and accepting, including your grandma.

When you met Michael realising you had lots in common, you had found your soul mate after a couple of false starts. It didn't take long for him to be a part of our family.

I love seeing how you both have a passion for DIY projects and are such a creative pair.

It shows through with the results you have achieved in making your beautiful home on 'Lilly May' your narrowboat.

As a family, we all had a fantastic day celebrating your marriage to Michael. An unforgettable day that highlighted your mutual passion by having all the guests arrive on a fleet of narrowboats. Off you both went on another adventure to Iceland and New York for your honeymoon.

I hope you are happy; I think you are enjoying your new job, which allows you to use all the skills learnt from your dad whilst working for the family business from age sixteen.

I hope you manage to travel more in the future, but for now, barging on the waterways with your darling little dog Pongo suits you just fine.

Love you always, and I hope you know your dad and I are always here for you

Your mum xx

Say a little Prayer – Aretha Franklin

The moment I wake up, before I put on my
makeup,
I say a little prayer for you
While combing my hair now, and wondering
what dress to wear now
I say a little prayer for you
Forever, forever you'll stay in my heart
And I will love you
Forever, forever we never will part
Oh, how I'll love you
Together, together that's how it must be
To live without you
Would only be heartbreak for me

To my daughter (youngest child)

Dear Katie (our princess),

I don't have to tell you in a letter how much you mean to me; I tell you often we are best friends as well as mother and daughter. We tell each other everything. I hope you like my choice of quote for you, the surprise song I sang to you on your wedding day, with the help of some special secretly prepared family members.

We have a shared love of reading and frequently swap books, spending far too much money in bookshops, much to the annoyance of our men.

When you came along to join your three brothers, I cannot describe the joy for the whole family; of course, your dad cried. You came into the world 'like a bullet'; you were number four, so no hanging around! That's when we knew our family was complete.

Our lives were always busy in our house with you four and me childminding. There never a dull moment, but I loved every minute of it and miss the madness now that dad and I are on our own.

You were never going to be a girly girl with three brothers, such a tomboy, but you held your own and kept up with them every step of the way.

The only time it bothered me that you were not girly was when your reception class had their Christmas play.

Previously I had two shepherds and a King; oh, how I wanted an Angel. You were such a sweet little blonde girl; I didn't expect anything less. You came running out of school so excited your teacher had chosen you to be a donkey! I took all your joy away by bursting into tears and rushing into school to speak to the teacher, who thought I had totally lost it! I got my angel, much to your disgust, and of course, you have never let me forget it, calling it child abuse.

You joined the village Rainbows and then Brownies and loved them both, but no way were you joining the Girl Guides. What learn to cook, sew or knit? No, thank you, only Scouts would do for you, with climbing, shooting, and archery being your favourite activities.

Scouting was a huge part of your life, with the highlight of being chosen to go to the World Scout

Jamboree in Sweden in 2011. You helped at beavers, became a cub leader and later an Explorer leader.

Scouting was where you met Gary, your first and only boyfriend when you were both Explorer leaders.

Roll on nine years, and you had the most stunning wedding to your first and only love. Blimey, no wonder Gary is just another member of our family; I can't believe we have put up with him all that time!!!

We speak almost every day, but I wish you lived a little nearer, I know forty-five minutes isn't far, but I hope you can move nearer to me in the future.

We all love your beautiful dog, Frank. He is a brilliant companion when Gary has to work away, and he is like your baby.

But I feel so blessed and excited about the next arrival to your family later this year (2022). Being able to help and advise you from my experience of giving birth and being a mum will mean so much. I didn't have anyone to help me when I became a mum with Richard. It can be daunting, my darling, but I will be by your side.

I will have to add a postscript to this book or a bonus chapter to update everyone.

You know that Dad and I think of Gary as another son, and we enjoy family times with his family too. "You did good, girl ", finding him, but we don't tell him too often. His head is big enough!

Thank you for helping me with this book. You know much more about writing than I do, having never done anything like it before. Lucky for me, you are currently doing a master's in English literature, so your help is invaluable.

I am so proud of the brilliant, strong, clever, beautiful woman you have become. I can't wait to share the next chapter of your life; I know you will make the most amazing mum.

Love you with all my heart,

Your mum and friend forever xx

"We'll be friends until we are old and senile.
Then we'll be new friends" – Unknown

To My Best Friend

Dear Donna,

Can you believe we've been friends for thirty years this year (2022)? Antony, your youngest, was just six weeks old when we both started working evenings at Matalan to help with our respective family finances.

We clicked, and the rest, they say, is history. Over the years, we have been there for each other through the ups and downs of life. I am so pleased that we have always managed to get together a few times a year, which usually involves cake. Always knowing we can call on each other at any time.

You were happy for me when I found my birth family, and we have talked through countless family issues over the years. I have always envied your fantastic relationship with your lovely mum, Sylvia, who I have become fond of over the years.

When my longed-for little girl Katie came along after three beautiful boys, you were the obvious choice as her godmother, alongside Auntie Margaret, who you now refer to as your friend. I think you bonded with her after spending the most surreal afternoon ever at Katies 'Hen do'. At eighty-two, I know she needed your support that afternoon; let's just say, 'what happens on the Hen Do stays on the Hen do, 'poor Auntie Margaret thought it was going to be a quiet afternoon tea!

Haven't we had some great times together over the years when the children were young? We used to go on lots of outings; I remember that time when we went to the woods, and Antony thought he could fly on his bike like ET. luckily, there were no broken bones.

Going to the theatre at least once a year before the pandemic hit was one of our shared pleasures, sometimes just us or with your mum and Katie; we all love the theatre. We have seen some great shows; we went to see 'Everybody's talking about Jamie' five days before the first lockdown. But the time we went to see

Aspects of Love at Milton Keynes Theatre that's the never to be forgotten one. We were running late because we couldn't find a parking space. We've always hated being late and tut when it's people in the row in front of us! We were trying to creep into the auditorium in the dark, nearly falling over. We ended up groping all the knees of the people in our row to find our seats which, of course, were right in the middle. We were laughing so much that we missed a quarter of the show. Thank God for the dark so that they couldn't see us properly. There were still some glares aimed in our direction in the interval.

I don't need to go into all the trials and tribulations of our families; we have shared them all.

I am looking forward to numerous years of outings, obviously with tea cake and perhaps the odd bit of knee groping.

Love you,

BFF Gaynor xx

"I've lived a life that's full. I travelled each and every highway and more, much more than this. I did it. I did it my way."

My Way Frank Sinatra your Funeral song

To my Birth Grandmother
(My Birth Dad's Mother)

Dear Grandma,

The family didn't let me meet you for a few years after we were reunited. I think they were worried about what you would say and if I could take it. You were indeed a 'speak your mind' kind of a woman.

We eventually met at Amy's 21st birthday meal in a pub; four years after I was back in touch with the family. You were certainly not a cuddly little grandma. You were a larger-than-life presence with a powerful voice who wanted to be the centre of attention and the Queen of the room.

The family pretended you weren't with them when you'd had a few drinks. You gravitated to any piano bashing out a tune like a showgirl.

You always did everything your way - 'My Way' played at your funeral. I think of it as your song, grandma.

The one-time dad brought you to see us at our home, and I had to go next door and apologise afterwards to our adjoining neighbours. We had an old upright piano for the kids to learn to play; oh my, you bashed it so hard and sang at the top of your voice. Dad spent the whole time telling you to calm down. But the kids loved every minute of it, and you were ecstatic.

I struggled to build a relationship with you for a few reasons; we couldn't get together very often as I had a demanding young family and a busy life, plus I found it difficult to forgive you for the past. You were the one person still alive who could have changed the course of my life back in 1963.

On your eightieth Birthday, the family got together to celebrate with you. We went to a pub and enjoyed a meal with all my children and their partners. Only Amy was missing because she was living in Germany at the time; you were in your element as the centre of attention.

My mum always said you had a few psychic vibes and that some of your weird predictions had come true over the years. I think you said I would come back one day, but the strangest one my family remember was concerning my son Chris.

You sat next to him on your birthday; you took his hand, looked him in the eyes and said:

"You won't become an actor, but I see you in prison."

Understandably this upset and shocked him, especially as he dreamed of becoming an actor; all his spare time was taken up with drama.

I predict you are looking down and laughing now because he didn't become an actor but a serving police officer; therefore, he has been to prison a few times!

My sisters have all sorts of stories about growing up with you and Grandad, who I never met, but the family tell me he was a lovely quiet man, and apparently, one of his frequent sayings to you went something like

"Put your brain into gear before opening your mouth, Eileen". I wish I had known him.

At least knowing you helped more piece's life's jigsaw slot into place.

RIP Grandma,

Your eldest granddaughter, Gaynor

You and Grandad (who I never met)

"Nieces are like sunshine on a rainy day" –
Catherine Pulsifer

To my two nieces
(Adopted sister Leesa's girls)

Dear Chloe and Eve,

I think I am your only Auntie, but life has thrown a few curveballs, so we are not as close as I wish we were.

When your mum and I were growing up, we had an up-and-down relationship. We were friends as little girls playing together, just twenty-one months between us. Our parents always said they wanted another girl as a playmate for me, but I think a boy would have challenged them too much. When we were young, the constant rivalry between us was typical, mainly caused by Beryl, who played us off against each other, making us quite competitive.

I am sure your mum has told you some stories about those times. Honestly, I don't remember much.

I have blocked a fair bit of it out. But as you know, we are great friends now.

Chloe, I think you have memories and embarrassing photos of growing up with my kids; as an only child then, you loved every minute of it, mucking in; and enjoying summers in our paddling pool. We saw quite a bit of you back then. But moving to Scotland when you were about eleven to live near Beryl and John meant we were not in touch for several years, leaving a hole in our lives. You still saw Richard when he visited your nanny and pappy. We missed all your teenage years up to age twenty-two, but as your Auntie, maybe that wasn't a bad thing!

When we all got back together, we clicked; it felt like you had never been away. You get on so well with your cousins as adults. It's a joy for me to see. You've shared some boozy nights out, crashing at our house; it has been brilliant getting to know you again.

At Katie's wedding, we met your partner, Sam; he fitted in well with the family and seemed to have quite a lot in common with Richard. We all have such busy lives, so we don't have family get-togethers that often, but we try to meet once a year. Last year in (2021) it was at Katie's wedding and this year (in 2022) for Eve's 21st. Next year (2023), Paul and I have a big birthday. Maybe soon there could be a wedding on the cards for you? (Need Auntie words with your Sam, I think!)

You and I frequently kept in touch during the Covid lockdown, trying to keep each other sane, as we were the two people in our families on furlough. I am so proud of you for setting up your own beauty business.

I know you will make a great success of whatever you do.

You are a beautiful, kind, caring young woman; I hope you know that. Even if I say you have the wrong hair colour, you know what I mean!!

Sending love,

Auntie Gaynor xx

Dear Evie,

I met you as a tiny baby before your family moved to Scotland, where you spent all of your childhood. When you came back into my life nine years ago, you were nearly a teenager, and your cousins were quite a bit older than you. Why would you want to get to know your crusty old Aunt? Plus, you still lived almost an hour away.

I don't feel I know you that well as a person; I know you had some teenage issues that you have overcome and a disastrous relationship, but things are looking great for you now. You love university life up north, with a new boyfriend and a part-time job.

It is great to get together on family occasions to catch up, but hard to hold proper conversations with all the prima donnas in our families taking over.

I hope we can get to know each other better as you get older, but I will still be crusty, of course!

Please know I am always here for you if you need anything or simply a bed for the night.

Good luck with your degree and future career; I hope all your dreams come true.

Big hugs,

Auntie Gaynor x

Baby Eve

Chloe and Sam

From Far-Left Michael, Eve, Sam and Chloe

Hannah Hall Photography

'To my Goddaughter' – by Grayson Blair

I felt so truly blessed
The day your parents asked me
The day I answered "Yes"
I promise through the years
With all of life's demands
My love for you will never change
I'm here with open arms
A commitment of faith
I bring to you
And to God above
Forever and always and through life's years
You'll always have my love

To My Goddaughters

Dear Grace and Willow,

You don't know each other and have never met, but you are both my godchildren, so you have that in common.

My friendship with your respective parents is entirely different. I hope I have been there for you both growing up; you are an amazing young woman. I have written you separate letters –

Dear Grace,

April 2022, I have just sent your 21st birthday card in the post; wow, where did those years go? So pleased you are enjoying university life and look forward to hearing about your achievements. I have loved learning about your progress over the years and trying my best to be there for you from a distance.

Your family moved to Derbyshire when you were still young because of your dad's job, so I didn't see you as often as I would have liked whilst you were growing up, but I kept in regular contact with your parents.

Your dad is probably my longest friend; I nearly said 'oldest,' but that would make him splutter and laugh! It's funny how he and I became friends at age thirteen and have been friends ever since we met at church which I often attended under sufferance. He went because he felt called, which, as it turned out, he was, later becoming a vicar.

I wonder what being brought up in a vicarage felt like for you; I am sure you have some stories to tell.

In your teens, you fought some personal problems, but your mum and dad supported you fully, and you have come through the other side a strong, caring, beautiful young woman; I am so proud of you.

Now that your mum and dad have moved back locally, I hope we can get together before too long. I hope you know I am always here if you need a shoulder, bed, cup of tea, or gin.

If you are interested, I can be bribed, usually with chocolate, to tell you a few stories of your dad from our youth.

With love,

Your Godmother (Auntie) Gaynor x

Dear Willow (my Goddaughter)

What an inspiration you are! I think you could write your own book about your experiences of transitioning.

I hope I have always supported you through the years; I am a true believer in being comfortable in your own skin, whatever it takes.

You are so brave to have gone down that route at such a young age, but you have fantastic parents supporting you every step of the way. I wasn't surprised to learn you felt you were a girl; I clearly remember buying 'my godson' sparkly plastic high-heel shoes for his sixth birthday.

I am sure this has not been easy for you; I hope you have kept notes through your journey to look back and see how far you have come and for any future family you may have.

Your mum and I hit it off so well back when she lived in our village. She is such a marvellous, bubbly, wacky lady. I met her as a friend of a friend, and then she became my children's babysitter, and of course, they loved her. Did she ever show you pictures of the mural she painted for Chris on his bedroom ceiling of

Charlie and the Chocolate Factory?

Not surprisingly, your northern parents were always going to head back that way wanting you and Simon to grow up in Yorkshire, which meant I didn't see much of you, but I kept in touch and lately, social media has helped enormously.

Your whole family started a new venture around the time of the Covid lockdown. What a brilliant success your new company has been. Nowadays, I wouldn't buy my soap and shampoo from anywhere other than 'Bee Clean Soaps!' My family must be sick of soap for Birthdays and Christmas. Is it better than socks? This venture may not be your long-term career, but I know you are enjoying working with your mum and brother for the time being. One of these days, I must come up North to see you at one of the fairs where you exhibit regularly.

I hope you know I love you and am so proud of the young lady you have become.

I am here if you ever need me. Keep being YOU always.

With love,

Your Godmummy Gaynor x

"In the end, you always go back to the people that were there in the beginning"
- Unknown

To my Birth Mum

Dear Mum,

I don't think I have told you how much I admire you for coping so well all these years.

Even, before the motto "Keep Calm and Carry on", was popularised, it has been your life's mantra.

You had no choice but to do just that, or you would not have survived all you have been through.

Younger generations go to counselling for their problems and traumas; you didn't have that choice. When they took me away from you, such things were unheard of and certainly not available.

Over the years, I think you have buried so much inside yourself; I still don't think you would be able to go to counselling now, even if it was offered.

But from my point of view, if you were able to write down your story, you would find it helpful to put your thoughts and feelings down on paper. I have found writing these letters so cathartic.

I would love to know more people's stories regarding adoption on any side of the triangle, and I would be honoured if people would send me their stories after they have read my book.

Everyone has a different perspective on adoption; no two stories will be the same. Take Leesa, for example. Although we grew up in the same house, our stories are so far apart; perhaps I can persuade her or let me write hers.

I know your life has never been easy, from parents who didn't have a happy relationship to everything that happened when you gave birth to me.

Your marriage to dad left much to be desired, ending in divorce. You have also had to cope with both Amy then Emma moving abroad. The sudden death of your sister hit you extremely hard just as you were about to retire and hoped to spend more time together; you had become much closer in later years. Then when the covid 19 lockdown came with no family nearby, living alone almost broke you.

Please know I love you and understand and try to help, but living an hour away, still working, plus being the matriarch of my large ever-growing family means everything is a balancing act.

The Movement for Adoption Apology is still trying hard to get justice for us all; things are still moving steadily in the background, with the reports being collated this summer, 2022.

I hope this ends well and we can share the victory together.

Sending love as always,

Your Cherie x

You and Dad at your wedding.

From far left: Paul, Me, You, Dad.

'My children didn't choose to be here, so they don't owe me anything, I chose to have them, I owe them everything"
– Elon Musk

To my Four Grown-up Children

"A family is the best team you could ever belong to."

Dear Team,

Or should I call you my famous five, four children and our dog Milo who thought he was a child too, joining in all your antics?

I love it when we all get together and reminisce with funny antidotes and banter; it's fantastic. Such a joy to know you all get on with each other and your respective partners. Our ever-expanding family will soon be getting too big for indoor get-togethers at home; I can see us using the village hall in the future.

All a parent can hope for is that their children had a happy childhood and still want to see their parents as adults. I think your dad and I have achieved that; I feel we are a tight unit.

You didn't grow up with other close family members, just your grandma, dad's mum; you saw quite a lot of her. She was a brilliant grandma to you all, treating Richard equally. She took you each in turn on day trips or short breaks and always arrived at our house with something for you she had found in a charity shop or car boot sale.

Luckily, she had excellent skills at making costumes for fancy dress parties and the many shows you performed in. Thank goodness she was an expert. Not my forte, was it?

Guys don't forget to occasionally contact grandma, even if sometimes she doesn't know who you are.

What a horrible illness dementia is.

I don't think you missed out on not having other grandparents around. Anyway, certain ones would have just created problems as they tried to in your early years. Aunties and Uncles came and went and were there in the background. I think because we lived in the same village all your childhood and teenage years, growing up with the same friends gave you security, which was all dad and I ever wanted for you.

I hope we have given you all "roots and wings."

Love you all to the moon and back.

Mum x

All of us in our Scouting and Guiding Uniform. A big part of family life. Dad: Scout Leader, Mum: Brownie Leader, Richard: Scout, Chris: Cub Scout, Adam: Beaver Scout and Katie: Honorary Brownie.

"If nephew and nieces were jewels, I would have the most beautiful gems ever" – Unknown

To My Nephew and Niece in the USA (My birth sister Amy's children)

Dear Evan and Sophie,

You are still young when I am writing this, but I hope you will get to read it one day.

This story is a small part of your history, too. Your grandma had a difficult time as a teenager; when I was a tiny baby, people told her she was too young to be a mother and couldn't look after me. Those people took me to live with another family. That meant I didn't grow up with your mummy and Auntie Emma as their big sister. I didn't even meet them until they were grownups.

Your life in America sounds amazing; having an American daddy and a British mummy gives you two different cultures.

Being so far away though, means you didn't get to know your British family. I know you would have great fun with my grandchildren, as they are your age group. I wish I could have been in your life as a hands-on auntie, but it is very common nowadays as countless families move around the world. Thank goodness we can keep in touch on Facebook and Facetime on special occasions.

Did you know our family had a funny chain of circumstances relating to the number sixteen? Your grandma had me at age sixteen, I had my Katie when your mummy was sixteen, and then your mummy had Evan when my Katie was sixteen. But my Katie has broken the chain because her baby is due later this year, and Evan, you are ten, but she may have more children; who knows, perhaps when you are sixteen, wouldn't that be funny?

I hope you can come on a trip to see us all, meet my grandchildren, your second cousins and make some memories to take back with you. After all, you are half-British yourselves, my darlings.

Big Hugs, Lots of love,

Auntie Gaynor x

"One minute your heart is bursting with love and pride as you watch your family grow, the next you are practically on your knees with exhaustion, Motherhood is a roller coaster'

– From Letters on Motherhood
Giovanna Fletcher

To Giovanna Fletcher. Podcaster, Writer and Queen of I'm a Celebrity Castle 2020

Dear Giovanna,

Your book 'Letters on Motherhood' inspired me to write my story for my family. You wrote to your boys, including your lovely husband Tom, in the form of letters. In your book, we learnt so much about your life through those beautiful letters, showing that you have an ordinary family life despite being a celebrity.

You are a brilliant advocate for all mothers, regardless of the age of their children.

It doesn't matter how old your children are; you will always be their mum, worry about them, care for them and want the best for them. That is what a mother's love is!

I have kept my copy of your book for my daughter to read when she becomes a mum, which will be later this year, God willing.

Thank you for sharing your family story, and I look forward to more updates over the years as your darling boys get older.

Thank you,

Gaynor x

"What's the difference between outlaws and in-laws? Outlaws are wanted!"

- @Dadsaysjokes

To the partners of my kids

Dear Rochelle, Katy, Gary and Mike,

I wrote your names in order of age, so we don't get any of that; who is the favourite business?

Sorry, you've got me as The Mother-in-Law, but I am happy to take all the old jokes as long I get the occasional nice comment, please.

Firstly, thank you all for taking that lot off my hands!

I still find it amazing there is no longer the "feeding of the five thousand' each mealtime. No piles and piles of washing and ironing; how the heck I survived all those flipping school shirts, I don't know! As for the food bill! Days after I've been shopping, there is still some food in the fridge; how strange is that? The house stays reasonably tidy (if we don't count Paul's input), the lights are now turned off, a TV somewhere is not constantly on, and sometimes I can hear silence.

Please don't send them back thanks; I couldn't cope:

Richard has too much energy and never sits still for a minute; I need peace these days.

Chris makes too much mess, plus our finances couldn't afford the electric bill.

Adam, well, if it's not a drama, then it's a crisis. Oh, the stress.

Katie, you are far too much like me; your dad has enough to put up with; he doesn't need it in duplicate.

"Did you hear about the cannibal that got married? He toasted his mother-in-law at the wedding. "

Boom, Boom

But in all seriousness, I am so pleased my kids picked you all; you are our family now. I love you like my own, and keep loving my kids as I do, please; that is all I ask.

Big hugs

From The Outlaw. x

From Left to Right Back Row: Christopher, Rochelle Richard's fiancée), Richard, Dad (Paul), Gary (Katie's Husband), Katie, Adam, Me (Mum), Michael (Adam's Husband), Katy (Christopher's Partner).

Front Row: Frank (Katie & Gary's Dog/Ring Bearer), Willow and Jaxon (Richard & Rochelle's Children).

Hannah Hall Photography

Toilet Rules –

If you lift it ...put it down

If it runs out.... Replace it

If you miss.... Clean it up

If you're finished....Flush, it

If it smells ... Spray, it

- Unknown but read in peoples loo's

To A Scouting Friend and
"Bog Squad" member

Dear Jeanette,

I couldn't have asked for a better "Bog Squad" teammate. People who know us from scouting still refer to you, me and Paul as the Bog Squad; what a laugh we had.

Who could believe we had such fun cleaning loos? What nutcases we are!

Funny how you just click with some people; You met Paul on the Cub Scout leadership team for

'Nailer' the big regional camp in 2006. I met you at that camp, where I was helping with our scout group, looking after the little darlings for the week.

We have been friends ever since. Finding out we both had mother issues meant we understood each other. Over the years, I have often made friends with ladies older than me; I guess it's that mother figure thing again.

Not that you are old enough to be my mum, of course, but not far off! You see, I can still be cheeky even when writing a letter!

A couple of years after that first camp, we were asked if we three would join the service team for county cub camp this time, and the bog squad came into existence. I won't go into detail about the daily routine of the infamous bog squad; let's just say extra-long rubber gloves, a plunger, an air freshener, and a strong constitution were essential.

What fun we had pulling the bog cart around camp, stopping off at lots of the cub group sites for a cup of tea, a cake, or a bacon butty; and yes, we did wash our hands! Fantastic camaraderie and our sense of humour kept us going.

We still laugh about Paul celebrating his '50' birthday weekend at camp doing bog squad duties, I offered him a weekend away, and he chose County cub camp, idiot!

I sent a request for his big birthday to the local radio station. The presenter phoned Paul on air to wish him a great birthday and ask about his plans. He laughed his socks off when Paul explained how he was spending his special birthday.

We decorated our tents, got a cake, and Paul was presented on stage in front of the five hundred or so people with a pink shower cap and toilet seat.

You, of course, had to try to top that for our silver wedding by painting a toilet brush silver putting a ribbon on it and handing it to us outside the church—cheers for that.

We often talk of how we miss those days, not the actual loo cleaning, just the laughs and fun.

I bet they never got such a great team as us again.

Our friendship worked even better when we discovered that your lovely husband Tom was in the same business as Paul. The stories they share, whoever said men can't natter like old women didn't know what they were talking about!

Thank you for your fantastic friendship. Here's hoping it continues for years to come, even though I like to remind you often you are so much older than me!!

Lots of love,

Gaynor x

"Did you hear the joke about covid-19? Never mind, I don't want to spread it around! "

To my Covid Walking partner

Dear Alma,

You are my old new friend; that sounds funny, but I knew of you as the mum of my school friend Elaine, who lived on the same street where I grew up. Back then, I knew you as Mrs O. I would never have called a friend's mum by their first name.

I knew you because you lived at the other end of the street and worked in the local Spar shop.

You only knew my parents as neighbours, not friends.

Being two years older, Elaine and I were not close friends. However, she was so helpful in looking after a few of us from our street when we started senior school, especially teaching us the school bus protocol. She would sit with me on the bus if I was sitting alone. My memories of her are that she was always kind to me.

When Covid 19 hit the world, it hadn't been long since you lost your husband and were now living alone. You realised you needed to get out of the house, deciding to walk the village circuit most days.

I also found lockdown hard on my own. Paul was able to continue working, but I got furloughed; I too, started walking because there are only so many Netflix series you can watch before going loopy.

We often crossed paths, usually going in opposite directions. At first, we greeted each other, moving on to a brief chat. In the coming weeks, we chatted for long that my fitness watch interrupted our conversations to remind me it was time to get going again.

Eventually, we arranged to start meeting so we could walk together, which has now become a regular weekly meeting. We walk together, putting the world to rights and learning about each other's families.,

I look forward to our Tuesday get-togethers.

You are the most positive person I know and a fantastic spritely lady. I walk fast, but you keep up with me easily even though you are in your eighties.

We now swap books regularly. You lent me your box set of 'Dexter' and got me addicted. You have become a proper friend over the last eighteen months. Thank you for helping me through a time of anxiety and stress. I am looking forward to many more chatty walks.

Love Gaynor x

"You'll achieve far more personal satisfaction trying to impress yourself than you will by trying to impress someone else - Kory Livingstone

To Me, Myself and I,

Why not write a letter to me? There are no rules when writing your own story. It's my story,

I can do what I like.

Dear Cherie,

This was the name you were given by your birth parents, with Ann as your middle name. But by six weeks old, it had been changed.

What would life have been like for Cherie, I wonder?

You would have grown up in a city, not a town, and had all your birth family around you. Would your parents have stayed together? Would they have had two more girls? The questions are endless.

But 'what ifs' are a useless waste of energy. Everything happens for a reason. You wouldn't have met the people you know; you would not be this person. You would be someone else entirely. So, no looking back and no regrets for the girl that wasn't to be.

Dear Gaynor,

Oh, how you have changed from the submissive girl growing up who felt inferior, insecure and different; you would hardly recognise her. You are now a happy, outspoken, confident woman. It has not always been easy and still isn't on occasion, but with the love from (your wonderful husband) Paul, your children and loads of amazing friends, you are transformed.

It has taken years and lots of life experiences, good and bad, to be in this perfect place you are in now.

Remember Gaynor; adoption doesn't represent who you are; it is just part of your life's challenge.

Of course, things will change in the future; they always do. But for now, at least, you are healthy and happy. Long may it continue. xx

Love from Me x

Suki and Me

Jasper and Me

"Someday when the pages of my life end. I know that my grandchildren will be one of my most beautiful chapters.'

To my Grandchildren; present and future

Dearest Darlings,

Who knows when you will read this? I may not be around, but please know I love you and will be with you always.

I hope you have enjoyed finding out more about me and a little bit of your family history.

I recommend keeping a diary of your life's significant events to look back on as you get old. Your children will appreciate it, I'm sure.

I wish I had asked my grandparents more about their lives, what they did in the two world wars, their jobs, and where they lived. It is a terrible shame, but eventually, family history disappears if it is not written down and passed on.

I could spend hours writing down valuable bits of advice for you all as you grow up, but one thing I know for sure, no one ever takes advice. You have to make your own mistakes in life and learn from them. So, go ahead and do it your way, but always do it to the best of your ability.

The other thing I am completely sure of is that love is key to everything. Love your family, your friends, your job and your life. If something does not feel right and you are not happy, change it until you become complete.

I hope I see you grow up, marry, and perhaps have your own children. Then I will feel satisfied that my life's work is complete.

With all my love,

Granny xx (or even great Granny) xx

Willow, Jaxon and new baby Ashdon

"I want to say thank you

To the rare few individuals in my life

Who have listened without judgement?

Spoken without prejudice

Helped me without entitlement

Understood without pretension

And loved me without conditions."

- Unknown

Thank You Letter

I feel the thank you note is a dying tradition; I grew up writing thank you notes for all my birthday and Christmas presents. I encouraged my children to write them too, with much moaning, of course.

Nothing is more pleasing than receiving thanks for a kind gesture or a gift. These days, it is usually by text or Facebook, but that's great because someone still took the time to thank you.

When Katie and Gary got married, three sets of Gary's family members sent Paul and I proper thank-you notes for the delightful time they had enjoyed. What a thoughtful thing to do. I have kept these in my special album.

I am taking this opportunity to say. Thank you for everything great in my life. The list could go on for pages, as I have been incredibly fortunate. I won't bore you with endless lists; it's like looking at someone else's holiday photos. Yawn yawn!

Thank you for taking the time to read my book; I know I bribed most of you, ha-ha!

Seriously though, a massive thank you for your support with this mad notion of mine.

However, I did think whilst writing this; that I had missed a small part of my life. I wanted to say a quick thank you to our pets. Over the years, we have had quite a few of various species, all making us laugh and then cry when they leave us. But they have taught us to care for something other than ourselves; they cheer us up when we are sad, even our chickens had their little quirks, and you always have a friend when things get tough.

We recently lost our little dog, Jasper. The pain is still raw; I miss him so much, and it is hard to say goodbye, but the time was right for him. The hole he has left will never be filled; he was part of our family and my trusted friend.

Thank you all for the wonderful memories. xx

"Write the story that's in your heart and not the one you think will pay the most money." -Brenda Jackson - author of Forged in Desire

To Sunday Times best-selling author Michael Heppell, all his group members and my newfound friends. Write that Book Masterclass of 2022, my accountability group 'Bestsellers' and Team 17

Dear All,

I cannot name you individually, but if you are included above, this letter is for you.

Unlike most of you, I did not have a burning passion for writing a book. I didn't think I was remotely capable of doing such a thing.

A failed eleven-plus followed by a lack of exam opportunities with the words, "You will only amount to being a cleaner ringing in my ears as I grew up. Write a book? Me? Impossible!

Then, one day up pops Michael Heppell's Write That Book programme; it leapt out at me from Facebook.

"I know it won't be for me, but I'll just take a look'. Eighteen months down the line.

And here it is … my book. Finished. Written. Success!

I have constantly been asking you amazing people for advice and support, which you all gave in bucket loads. This writing experience has given me confidence in myself, some of which I had lost due to Covid 19.

I have loved the process, but more importantly, I have made lifelong friends. The guidance and help from you all has been phenomenal.

Various people over the years have made a flippant remark to me, "your story would make a good book", which sometimes got me thinking, I wonder if people would want to hear my story, or would someone want to write it for me?

Then randomly up pops Michael Heppell's Write that Book page on Facebook, so I thought, I will just have a look to see what that is all about, never expecting to get entirely involved and 'write that book'!

But on the 'flip side', get it? I am 'skint', because how could I not buy most of the fantastic books you amazing people have written? My book wish list is full to bursting, and so are my bookshelves.

What an incredible bunch of compassionate people you all are. I am honoured to call you all my friends.

With love and newfound <u>Author</u>ity (ha-ha).

Gaynor Cherieann

Nothings Gonna Change My Love for You –
Glen Medeiros (Our song)

If I had to live my life without you near me
The days would all be empty
The nights would seem so long
With you, I see forever oh so clearly
I might have been in love before
But it never felt this strong
Nothing's gone change my love for you

To My Husband

Darling Paul,

I thought I better finish (well, almost) with a final letter
to you.

Our children have grown up having fun about the
pecking order in the family. Saying who they think is
the favourite and why, which they claim, constantly

changes! When a new partner joins our family, the order gets moved around, sometimes including the pets. Our delightful children arrive at our house, shout, put the kettle on, raid the fridge, and then spend time inspecting the photo wall and counting the number of times they are pictured in the various photographs. If there is not an equal split, God forbid!

Hence, following this family tradition, I thought I had better write another letter to you as some people in this book may have more letters!!

I don't have much to say in this letter as I feel I have said it already, and the reader can only put up with so much of my waffle!

Thank you for being you and loving me for who I am (and our daughter will ask whether I counted the times you have cried whilst reading this?). Not that you read books; you are proud to tell people you have read just two in your life, but you better read this one or else!

With all my love forever,

Gaynor xx

"A writer only begins a book. A reader finishes it."- Samuel Johnson

To you, The reader

Dear Reader,

My final letter, but there may be a bonus one if you contact me.

Thank you for taking the time to read this book. I hope I have inspired you to write your own story for your family. Or perhaps you have remembered those old diaries hidden away somewhere and feel the urge for a trip down memory lane.

I would love to hear your family's stories, especially if they have an adoption twist. It is an incredibly sensitive subject with loss at the heart of the story for all involved. I am considering compiling other people's adoption stories into a book and would be honoured if you shared yours with me. The details of how to get in touch with me will be at the back of the book.

Everyone's story is unique; I have found that telling mine has been incredibly cathartic and surprisingly enjoyable. I would love to encourage everyone to write down or record theirs before it disappears forever.

Thank you for taking the time to read my letters.

Yours faithfully, sincerely and gratefully

Signing off with love,

Gaynor x

STOP THE PRESS

LATE ADDITION NEWS:-

I am delighted to announce the safe arrival of a beautiful granddaughter Elsie Cherieann on 31st October 2022.

Our wonderful new addition to the family arrived five days early weighing 7lb 3 oz (in old money) congratulations to Katie and Gary, not forgetting Frank (their dog).

I cannot wait to get to know her and watch her grow up.

With love Granny

May you touch the stars and reach for the moon. May you grow up with kindness, peace and love and may your life be blessed with amazing experiences.

Welcome to the world Elsie it has been waiting for you.

References

Letters On Motherhood by Giovanna Fletcher

Dear Fatty by Dawn French

Quotes from internet sites:
quotesgram.com/parade.com/Shutterfly.com

Song Lyrics – Lyrics.com

Hannah Hall Photography provided some photos; permission was granted.

All other photographs are from the Author's personal collection.

Contact

If you have enjoyed this book, I would love to hear from you. Please feel free to get in touch.

Please help me by posting a review on my website or Amazon (An Adoptees Journey -Letters of my life).

Website: gaynorcherieannauthor.wordpress.com

Email: gaynorcherieannauthor@outlook.com

Facebook: gaynorcherieannauthor

Instagram: gaynorcherieannauthor

Everyone has a story to share and remember. I would encourage you to write yours down for the future.

As you now know I love receiving a handwritten letter and would be delighted if you obliged. Get in touch via email for my address.

Any personal stories about adoption you share with me I will keep in a special place. I may, with your permission, compile them into another book in the future.

Thank you,

Gaynor

Acknowledgements

This book would not exist without the help and encouragement of the following people:

Most importantly, my family for their endless support and love. You are my world.

Katie, my ramblings would not be a book without your assistance and advice with everything book related.

Paul, for understanding, putting up and believing in me and helping with wording (not the spelling!)

Gary, for IT assistance,

Rochelle, for the front cover photograph.

Everyone I have written to - these letters are to thank you for being you.

Write that Book gang 2021 & 2022, The Masterclass 2022, and my accountability group Bestsellers; you have been so supportive.

Michael Heppell, what an inspiration. Thank you for the care in writing my Foreword.

Mathew Bird, I couldn't have got here without your advice and brilliant typesetting skills.

Anna Anderson, a fellow adoptee, you understood my story and were able to edit my book with love and care.

Sue Cox and Ann O'Brien, for being my First Readers and giving me your precious time and helping this to become a reality.

Elaine Canham (Northampton Adult Learning), you set me on the path of using letters to tell my story.

Thank you to BBC via Duncan Kennedy and The Daughters of the Holy Spirit for the use of Photographs

About the Author

Gaynor Cherieann is an adoptee from Northamptonshire, born in 1963. A mother of four and a granny to four children, two dogs and two cats. She has been married for thirty-three years to her ever-supportive husband.

In 2021, Gaynor was interviewed by BBC presenter Duncan Kennedy for his documentary - "If You Love Your Baby".

In this documentary, he shows why there is a much-needed Movement for an Adoption Apology from the British Government due to the decades of women shunned by society and forced to give up their babies against their will. Gaynor expresses to Duncan her feelings about the fact that her mother was forced to give her away.

Gaynor is an avid supporter of the Movement. She believes these terrible practices affected millions of women and their children, including herself and her mother.

Her unique memoir is written through the power of letters for her family and herself to reflect on and keep in their hearts forever. Many stories of adoption and its impact on families are lost forever, now is her chance to save hers.

Printed in Great Britain
by Amazon

17373983R00129